DOUGLAS JUMBO'S
THE
GLOBEMASTER

D0814120

by
Anthony J. Tambini

BRANDEN PUBLISHING COMPANY
17 Station Street Box 843
Brookline Village, MA 02447

Library of Congress Cataloging-in-Publication Data

Tambini, Anthony J.
  Douglas jumbo's : the Globemaster / by Anthony J. Tambini.
    p. cm.
  Includes bibliographical references and index.
  ISBN 0-8283-2044-6 (alk. paper)
  1. C-124 (Transport plane)
  2. C-47 (Transport plane)
  3. C-17 (Jet transport)
  I. Title,
  UG1241.T7T35   1999
  623.7'465--dc21   99-12755
                                           CIP

BRANDEN PUBLISHING COMPANY
17 Station Street
Box 843 Brookline Village
Boston MA 02447

CONTENTS

4 A. J. Tambini

INTRODUCTION

The world was mesmerized in February of 1969 when the Boeing 747 Jumbo Jet took to the skies on its first test flight. Lost in history is the fact that in 1945 Douglas Aircraft test pilots took off on a test flight in an aircraft that set the standard for the jumbo aircraft that would follow. Only a very limited number of these aircraft, the C-74 Globemaster I, were produced. However, its successor, the C-124 Globemaster II, followed in the lead set by the C-74 and established itself as the first truly heavy lift and outsized cargo transport to enter USAF service.

The C-124's first flight was in 1949, it was retired from active duty in 1974. Not much has been documented of Globemaster II's history during its extensive years of service with the Military Airlift Command. Carrying heavy cargo of unusually large dimensions was a role this aircraft was designed for, and performed exceptionally well in. Unfortunately, due to its relatively slow cruising speed, modest ceiling, and ungainly looks, it never caught the public's eye as other less capable but ascetically appealing planes did. One designed-in feature of the Globemaster I & II, not widely known, is the fact that they were capable of carrying 200 fully equipped combat troops. This in an era when civilian and military transports were carrying by and large less than half this number of passengers.

The Globemaster II was the last of what USAF technicians affectionately called a "flight engineers airplane." A flight engineer on the propeller driven Globemaster performed a wide range of duties that kept him, (there were no female flight engineers assigned to these airplanes), continually busy in-flight. Adjusting engine settings, plotting performance parameters, inspecting the aircraft, and even climbing out into the wings to repair the engines in-flight were all part of the duties of reciprocating engine driven Globemaster flight engineers. The term "Shaky" was often used to affectionately refer to the Globemaster II. The term stuck almost from the start. Its four huge R-4360 engines producing 3,000 plus horsepower per engine, large 17 foot diameter propellers, and unpressurized interior, set up some unusual airframe harmonics that caused it to shake and rattle during flight.

This book is intended to be a Globemaster trilogy. However, it is primarily the story of the Globemaster II. The reason is simple, very few Globemaster I's were produced, and the Globemaster III has yet to make its mark in the annals of Military Airlift.

Chapter I
GENISIS: THE GLOBEMASTER I

It would not be considered a stretch of the imagination to assume that military planners during the Second World War realized that the transport of men and materials by ship was at best hazardous, at worse a deadly venture. The German submarine threat to shipping convoys during the early war years created unacceptable losses in both men and equipment. The tonnage sunk by the enemy was staggering throughout the first few years of the war. Ship convoys departing the east coast of the Americas required an escort of destroyers and aircraft that could have been utilized in other operational theaters. Weather in the North Atlantic was another factor that at times impeded the flow of convoys to our allies across the sea. The impact of lost mariners and their ships was devastating to American morale. The loss of fathers and sons to the unseen threat of the submarine resulted not only in a morale issue, it also placed a drain on the construction of combat vessels, as replacements for each sunk cargo ship would be required. The transport of at least some of the high value outsized cargo by air would have been of great significance to the war effort had aircraft specifically designed for the task been available.

Air transport at the start of the war was if nonexistent, then outdated. The famous lifeline into China from Burma, flying the "Hump" was initially accomplished with the Douglas C-47. Originally designed as a civilian passenger aircraft, it was not well suited to carry the huge loads required for the logistical support of allied forces in China. As with the Atlantic ship convoys, the air lifeline into China was fraught with hazards such as mountain peaks that reached almost to the limit of the aircraft's performance envelope. Weather was another critical factor in these air operations, which took its toll in lost lives. The requirement for flying supplies into China started with the American Volunteer Group (AVG), the famous Flying Tigers, formed to assist the Chinese fight external aggression. In 1942 Colonel Caleb Haynes formed what was officially called the Assam-Burma-China (ABC) Ferrying Command. The Command was tasked to supply fuel and ammunition to the AVG, and was initially provided only two C-47 aircraft. Air supply was required after the enemy had cut the overland supply road, which was an 800 mile route from Kunming in China to Lashio and Mandaly in Southern Burma. The C-47's capacity in these flights was limited in order to allow the aircraft to climb to a sufficient altitude to clear the 16,000 foot peaks of the Himalayas that exist in the North of Burma. Near the end of 1942, the Ferry Command was melded into the newly created Air Transport Command. By early 1943, the Command was delivering approximately 2,500 tons of supplies each month into China. The Curtiss C-46 Commando had by then entered service and in addition to the C-47, was also flying supplies "Over the Hump." By mid 1945, with the C-54 Skymaster taking over most of the deliveries, the airlifters of the ATC were delivering 71,000 tons of supplies monthly. In the end, 1314 airmen had lost their lives delivering over three quarters of a million tons of supplies into China over the "Hump." Quite triump for both the men and the equipment they used flying these very dangerous missions.

Because of these and many other factors, military planners in the War Department were well aware of the need for developing a large aircraft capable of transporting men and material long distances rapidly. The delivery of the Douglas Skymaster and Lockheed Constellation while welcomed did not actually increase airlift capabilities adequately enough to address the concerns of the military. Both aircraft were considerably more capable than the C-46 and C-47 that preceded them but none were able to carry heavy outsized cargo such as tanks, half-tracks, trucks, and such. Airdrop capabilities were also limited throughout the war. All could drop paratroops and air deliver cargo; however, a quantum leap was required to adequately insert and support combat forces. This was a lesson learned during campaigns in both operational theaters during the war. Indeed, during the D-Day invasion of continental Europe in June of 1944 vast armadas of transport planes and towed gliders were required to insert combat forces into France. In the China-Burma-India Theater of Operations air assaults also required transports and towed gliders. In the early morning hours of 6 March 1944, 26 C-47's with GC-4A towed gliders took off in an effort to support British efforts to stem the advance of enemy forces into Burma. This operation, code named *"Broad-way"* was to have inserted combat troops and equipment into a jungle clearing 165 miles behind enemy lines. Of the 52 gliders that participated in the operation, only 37 arrived at the drop zone. The 15 missing crashed due to overloading and broken tow ropes. Of those arriving in the drop zone, only 3 landed without damage.

The destiny of air transport changed with a contract award to the Douglas Aircraft Company of Long Beach California for the construction of the XC-74 Globemaster I. The XC-74 was originally designed by Douglas as a civilian airliner. The civilian version, designated as the Douglas Model 415A, was to be a greatly enlarged version of the Douglas DC-4, (the military's C-54 Skymaster). In 1945, Pan American World Airways placed an order with Douglas for 26 of the civilian version, to be called the DC-7, for its transatlantic air routes. The airliner was to be pressurized and outfitted with accommodations for a crew of 10 and a maximum passenger loading of 108 for day time flying and 76 for night flights. The passenger compartment was to be outfitted with a lounge bar, dining area, and sleeping cabins for night flights. The installation of sleeping cabins would have accounted for the difference in the amount of passengers carried between day and night. Although not a new or novel idea, in-flight sleeping accommodations were later incorporated into airliners such as the Douglas DC-6 "Dayplane Sleeper", Boeing B-377 Stratocruiser, and much later into some versions of the Boeing 747. Unfortunately, Pan American canceled the DC-7 order in the latter part of 1945. The Douglas DC-7 designation would resurface in the 1950's as the successor to the DC-6.

Douglas started preliminary design work in January of 1942 on a military version of the Model 415A, which was called the Long Range Heavy Lift Transport. The Army Air Forces designated the Model 415A as the XC-74 Globemaster, and directed Douglas to build 50 of the giant transports. The XC-74 differed slightly from the proposed commercial version, primarily in the fact that the pressurized interior proposed for the civilian version was deleted for the military transport. The first USAAF experimental XC-74 flew from the Douglas facility at the Long Beach, California airport on September 5, 1945. The aircraft was 31 feet longer than the C-54 (DC-4) Skymaster, and would be 24 feet longer than the then proposed C-118 (DC-6) Liftmaster. It was designed to carry a 50,000 pound payload 3,400 miles. The DC-6A, which was developed after the C-74 was flying, could only carry 28,000 pounds 2,900 miles. The Globemaster I had laminar flow wings with full span fowler flaps. One of aircraft's more unusual external features were twin blister type canopies mounted on the top forward section of the fuselage. The left blister served as a cockpit canopy arrangement for the pilot and the right for the co-pilot. Both pilots shared the common flight deck with the rest of the crew. It was typical of the times to design a canopy type arrangement onto large aircraft. Canopies were incorporated into the XB-42 and XB-43 experimental bombers. A single large blister type canopy was incorporated into the B-36 bomber, the B-47 was produced with a blister type canopy, and finally the YB-52 originally came out with a design closely resembling the B-47 canopy.

The aircrew of the Globemaster I consisted of a pilot, copilot, flight engineer, navigator, radio operator, and loadmaster. Overall dimensions were huge compared to other transport aircraft of this era. The wing span stretched 173 feet, 3 inches, its length was 124 feet, 2 inches, and its height was 43 feet, 9 inches. It had an empty weight of just over 86,100 pounds and a loaded gross weight of 172,000 pounds, which made it the largest air transport of its time. It was powered by four huge Pratt and Whitney R-4360-27 (later upgraded to the -49) Wasp Major radial air cooled engines that delivered 3,250 horse power each. Attached to the engines were 17 foot diameter Curtis Electric propellers. These four bladed propellers were capable of being "feathered", that is when the engine was shut down in flight the propellers could be streamlined with the airflow to prevent them from rotating, and thus creating unwanted drag on the aircraft. They also incorporated a reversible pitch system, which provided additional stopping power upon landing. Maximum speed of the aircraft was 325 mph. With the engines adjusted to a 64% power setting, the aircraft could cruise at 296 miles per hour at 20,000 feet. It had a maximum unrefueled range of 3,500 miles. The XC-74's maximum range was 7250 miles, enough to circle the earth with only two servicing stops. In 1946 an XC-74 was test flown at a gross weight of 86 tons, which was an unheard of feat for that time frame. In the troop transport configuration it was designed to carry 200 passengers, and as an air ambulance it was designed to carry a maximum of 127 litter patents.

The aircraft was also designed to allow maintenance to be accomplished on the engines while in flight. The flight engineer could enter the lower crawlway compartment, under the main cabin deck, and climb out into the wing to the engine. Once at the engine the engineer could lower a firewall access door and perform a variety of maintenance. This is discussed in detail in the next chapter.

In September of 1946 the USAAF generated a plan to test the new aircraft. The 554th AAF Air Base Unit at Memphis Municipal Airport, Memphis, Tennessee was selected to conduct an operational test of the aircraft. On 5 September the 554th Air Base Unit C-74 squadron was activated. The operational test was designed to test the aircraft for non-scheduled, non-stop flights from Fairfield-Suisun, (later renamed Travis Air Force Base), to Washington, DC. The flights would be cargo only, no passengers were authorized. This project was designed to be a "shakedown' of the aircraft prior to entering operational service. Training of personnel to conduct this test was to have been accomplished by aircrews and technicians initially C-74 trained at Wright Field in Dayton, Ohio and also at the Douglas facility at Long Beach, California. Approximately 30 transcontinental flights were planned, and at the end of the project the following was to be assessed:

The need for any special loading equipment associated with the new aircraft.
- A.   Loading techniques and procedures developed or followed.
- B.   Characteristics of the cargo compartment for loading and unloading.
- C.   Tie-down facilities within the aircraft.
- D.   Information on air-evacuation.
- E.   All other valuable data concerning loading and unloading of freight and mail.

F. Comments of future use as a combination cargo and passenger aircraft.

G. Man hours and time required to complete loading and unloading.

Also part of the test was a requirement to gather all technical data concerning maintenance difficulties encountered, to record man hours required to accomplish inspections, engine changes, other maintenance, establish emergency procedures to be used in the future, and to determine handling characteristics of the aircraft. One additional item that was considered extremely important was to assess how fast the 300 hour servicing could be accomplished on the R4360-27 engines installed on the aircraft.

Pilots and Co-Pilots assigned to the project were to have a minimum of 2,000 hours of multi-engine flying. Flight Engineers were to be selected based on being "the most highly qualified." Check out times for the pilots was to be a minimum of 12 hours, which consisted on six day and four night landings. Flight Engineers would receive 20 hours of panel instruction. One item of interest was the fact that the operational plan stated that "the aircraft is easier to fly than the C-54, the pilot and co-pilot will have even less to do. The only new thing is reverse pitch on the propellers."

On September the 13th, 1946, an aircrew was sent to pick up the project's first C-74, serial number 42-65406, at the Douglas facility in Long Beach. The crew consisted of the pilot - Colonel Cassady, co-pilot - Lt. Col. Moomaw, flight engineers - SSGT's Cotterman and Swanson, navigator - Capt. Pullen. Also along on the flight were two additional relief pilots - Captain's Shubrick and Huddleson. After two check flights at Long Beach Airport, the aircraft departed on the 19th of

September. The flight from Long Beach California to Memphis Tennessee took 7 hours and 20 minutes.

On 4 October 1946, the squadron was transferred to the 1103rd AAF Base Unit at Morrison Field, West Palm Beach, Florida, where testing continued. The first highlight of the testing came on October 24. Test mission number six was a flight from Morrison to Marietta, Georgia to pick up ten jeeps, which was considered quite a feat for the time. All 10 jeeps were loaded into the aircraft using the elevator loading platform. The jeeps were to be used by the unit back at Morrison. The aircraft departed Marietta with a gross weight of 140,453 pounds.

The second aircraft, serial number 42-65411 arrived the first week of January of 1947. On January 14th 1947 aircraft 406 took off from Miami Airport on a flight to Panama. Not long after take-off an engine throttle control cable broke forcing the flight engineer to shut the engine down in-flight and feather the propeller. The aircraft returned to Miami, where the broken cable was replaced. After the repairs, the aircraft took off again, bound for Panama. Just after take-off, at 200 feet, black smoke started to pour out of the number 4 engine. The aircraft again returned to Miami, and made an uneventful emergency landing. The third aircraft, serial number 42-65409 arrived at Morrison on the 19th of January. The next day this aircraft flew to Miami Airport with a new engine for aircraft 406.

Aircraft 42-65412 and 42-65413 arrived Morrison on the 2nd of February 1947. With the addition of these two aircraft the operational test squadron had five C-74's assigned. On February 27, 1947, one of the assigned aircraft departed Morrison Field for Borinquen Field, Puerto Rico carrying the largest payload for any aircraft up to that time, 31,000 pounds. The non-stop flight was 1,032 miles, which was accomplished in three hours and 55 minutes.

The end of the operational test project generated a report that contained the following information:

"Experience gained indicates an urgent and pressing need for continued experiment in larger and larger transport aircraft to move vast quantities of men and supplies in minimum time should another conflict develop. The C-74 test squadron has fully demonstrated the capabilities of this type aircraft during this operational test. The problem of handling an aircraft which weighs, fully loaded, in the range of between 145,000 - 165,000 pounds presents maintenance and traffic problems which must be approached from a new angle. We faced that initial loss of time and efficiency simply because the operating crews, principally loading crews at terminals where the traffic was heaviest, were still thinking in terms of loading a C-54 type aircraft. Many times not enough trucks or equipment were available to rapidly load and unload the large quantity of cargo carried. Experiments with this aircraft indicate that it can be handled on the same airports from which we are now operating the C-54. Its minimum landing roll of 2000 feet is well within the limitations of most airports from which any sizable aircraft can operate. Its take-off and 3 engine climb at the present gross weight is well within the margin of safety for this type of equipment". Clearly the conclusions in this report set the stage for the C-124 and indeed all large transports that followed the historic Globemaster I.

An interesting note in this report states that the R4360-27 engine will undoubtedly serve the Air Force successfully for large type aircraft, both transport and bomber, during the development phase of jet and gas turbine power units of 3000 to 5000 horsepower. It appeared to be obvious in 1947 that the jet era was upon us and that the R4360 would probably be the largest aircraft piston engine developed for service use.

As with the end of most major military conflicts the United States has been involved within recent times, the end of the Second World War heralded calls for drastic reductions in military expenditures. The original contract order for 50 Globemaster I's was significantly reduced to 14. These 14 aircraft were delivered to the USAF for service in the Military Air Transport Service (MATS).

The Berlin Airlift of 1948 (Operation Vittles) added further impetus to the requirement for a large cargo aircraft. The Soviet closure of all ground transportation into West Berlin on June 22, 1948 created conditions that required the western sections of the city to be supplied solely by air. The airlifter fleet consisted of 300 U.S. aircraft, primarily Douglas C-47 Sky-trains and C-54 Skymasters, and a fleet of 101 Royal Air Force aircraft, which included RAF bombers, some seaplanes and C-47 Dakota's. Round the clock flights into the city provided the residents of West Berlin with life's basic necessities.

The Airlift started on June 26, 1948 and was terminated on September 30, 1949 when a frustrated Soviet Union again allowed ground access into West Berlin. The two hundred million dollar airlift delivered 2,325,000 tons of supplies requiring close to 190,000 flights culminating in over 586,000 flight hours. Thirty-one Americans died in 12 crashes during the airlift.

Clearly an aircraft specifically designed for air cargo was required. Had the C-74 gone into full production the same amount of tonnage delivered daily into West Berlin could have conceivably been delivered with fewer aircraft. Indeed, during the Berlin Airlift, several C-74's took over C-54 routes and operated flights from Alabama to Frankfurt, Germany with a refueling stop in the Azores. This freed up more C-54's to fly the Berlin Airlift. Globemaster I's also supported West Berlin in other ways, for example in August of 1948 a C-74, in two trips, flew in 57,500 pounds of heavy engineering equipment to Tempelhof Airport in West Berlin which was used to construct a new runway.

On November 18, 1949, a C-74 set a significant milestone by becoming the first aircraft to carry more than 100 people across the Atlantic Ocean. On that date a Globemaster I took off from Alabama loaded with 108 passengers and crewmembers and flew onto England. The significance of this event can be understood by comparing the passenger loading of other aircraft of this time frame. For example, the C-54 Skymaster, which first flew in early 1942, had a main cabin seating capacity of 26. The postwar civilian version, the DC-4, was originally designed for a maximum passenger capacity of 44, with a 5' man crew. The DC-6, which first flew in December 1947 was originally designed for a passenger load of 58 with a 4 man crew.

During April of 1951 a Military Air Transport Service C-74, (MATS flight 5409), developed a problem that was more or less typical of reciprocating engine transports of the day. While enroute from Lages Field, the Azores to Kindley Air Force Base, Bermuda the aircraft experienced problems with one of its four engines. The aircrew was forced to shut the engine down and feather the propeller. The crew, concerned with a forced landing into the water, a "ditching", requested escort assistance into Kindley. The 7th Air Rescue Squadron from Bermuda dispatched an SB-17G (a World War Two B-17 bomber modified for search and rescue) as an escort aircraft. The rescue aircraft was radio vectored to the Globemaster, established radio contact, and eventually a visual intercept was accomplished. The remainder of the flight was uneventful, with a safe landing being made in Bermuda. In the 1940's and 50's, in-flight engine shutdowns occurred regularly, which at times required the crew to jettison cargo in an effort to make the aircraft as light as possible to sustain flight with one or more engine's shutdown. Unfortunately there were times when this type of effort proved futile and the aircraft would make an unscheduled water landing.

In 1954, the 1703rd Air Transport Group (Heavy) at Brookely Air Force Base, Alabama was assigned operational responsibility for all C-74's. This unit was instrumental in providing logistics support to the Tactical and Strategic Air Command's. Globemaster I's from the base took part in supporting the first deployment of Republic F-84 Thunderjets across the Pacific Ocean. C-74's from Brookely also supported the movement of aircraft from the US to Algeria in Northern Africa. In 1954, C-74's from the 1703rd Air Transport Group participated in Operation Embryo Eyelet. This operation required the airlift of ten T-6 trainer aircraft from Kelly Air Force Base, Texas to Montevideo, Uruguay.

By July of 1955 all of the C-74's had been removed from active service due to an extremely low utilization rate of 4 hours. This low utilization rate coupled with the fact that only 14 were manufactured resulted in significant logistics problems supporting such a small fleet of aircraft. They were also suffering reliability problems by this time, and at the time of deactivation they were grounded for faulty fuel selector valves and defective elevator attachment pins. The remaining aircraft were placed in permanent storage, and eventually destroyed. Fortunately no C-74's were lost during their years of service. Their were reports that 3 of the 14 aircraft were turned over for civilian use, and were operated into the early 1960's by the Panamanian airline Aeronaves de Panama. However, discussions with the Panamanian Directorate of Civil Aviation has proven these claims false. The Civil Aviation Department provided a listing of 46 Douglas aircraft that have resided in Panama over the years. Only one of the 46 was a C-74 (Panamanian registration HP-367/USAF serial number 42-65408). These previous reports stated that one of the reported C-74's delivered to Panama carried Panamanian registration number HP-379. This registration number was actually assigned to a Cessna Model 180F. The other aircraft was reported to carry registration HP-385. The Director of Civil Aviation reportedly has no record of this registration number being issued to a Douglas product. One of the 14 (serial number 42-65406) was converted into the prototype YC-124A configuration, with the serial number changed to 48-795.

The Globemaster I proved the viability and need for a heavy lift military transport. It may well have set the stage for all future "Jumbo" transports that followed. The operational testing and actual transport missions that the C-74 flew resulted in the Air Force's decision to develop even larger transport aircraft. The retirement of the aircraft came at a time when its name sake, the Globemaster II, was entering service in large numbers.

Summary of Selected Aircraft Systems:
Cargo Loading Operations:

Loading Platform - Cargo could be loaded utilizing a loading platform located under the aircraft amidships. This loading platform made up a section of the main cabin flooring, and used two on-board overhead traveling electric cranes in the main cabin for the lifting operation. The cranes had a combined capacity of 16,000 pounds. This loading method was incorporated into the C-124 Globemaster II without much change, and is discussed in detail in the next chapter of this book.

Fuselage Cargo Door- A large cargo loading door was incorporated into the left side of the fuselage just inboard and forward of the inboard (#2) engine. The door provided enough area to load vehicles slightly larger than a jeep into the aircraft. Cargo could be lifted into the aircraft through this door with the use of a portable hoist. The forward cargo door was a novelty in the C-74's day, as most other cargo aircraft incorporated rear cargo loading doors. Advantage of the forward loading cargo door was that aircraft such as the DC-3, C-46, Lockheed Constellation, etc. had fuselage's that tapered at the rear of the aircraft. This limited the size of cargo that could be loaded into these aircraft. The large forward cargo loading door would later be incorporated into most modern commercial cargo jet aircraft such as the freighter version of the Douglas DC-8.

Flight Control System:

The C-74 had a conventional flight control system. This meant that the pilot's controls on the flight deck were directly linked, through a series of cables and pulleys, to the control surfaces. One exception to this was the aileron system. An aileron hydraulic boost was provided to reduce pilot forces. An on/off control switch on the pilots electrical control panel controlled the operation of the boost system. This was an effort to maintain structural safety, the boost limited the aileron "throw" or travel at high speeds. Also provided to the pilot was an Emergency Boost Release Lever. This lever was located on the pilots central control pedestal and was used for emergency disengagement of the aileron boost system. The boost system could not be reengaged in flight once the boost release lever was pulled. Reengaging the system required a maintenance technician to reconnect a control linkage in the lower aft cargo compartment. The ailerons were designed to move down in conjunction with the trailing edge flaps, thus forming the "Full Span Flap System". This system allowed, in effect, the entire trailing edge of the wing to become one large trailing edge flap.

Fuel System:

The C-74 carried 11,100 gallons (approximately 66,000 pounds) of standard aviation gasoline, grade 115/145. Fuel was carried in six wing tanks, two outboard wing tanks, two inboard wing tanks and two auxiliary wing tanks. Refueling the aircraft was a time consuming and arduous task, as the flight engineer or mechanic was required to enter the main cabin, climb onto the top of the wing and refuel each wing tank individually.

As can be expected, refueling the aircraft during inclement weather could be risky, especially when the wings were covered with ice, wet from rain, or with the sun beating down on a silvery extremely hot wing. During the early 1950's the "single-point" refueling system came into use. This method, which was incorporated into later versions of the C-124, allowed for the flight engineer or mechanic to attach the refueling hose to a single point on the underside of the aircraft and refuel all fuel tanks at one time. The system would automatically shut-off when the aircraft was completely serviced with fuel, or a predetermined fuel quantity could also be controlled with this new system.

In-flight control of the aircraft fuel system was the responsibility of the flight engineer. Selection of wing tank fuel valves was accomplished mechanically. To open or close a fuel tank valve, controlling the fuel distribution within the wings and flow to the engines, the flight engineer would push or pull on the selected fuel control lever mounted at the engineers control table. Each of the 6 tank selector levers were connected mechanically, via a set of steel cables and pulleys, to their respective fuel valve's. Pulling the lever to shut off the flow of fuel from the tank mechanically moved the internal mechanism of the valve to the closed position. Pushing the lever reversed the motion and opened the valve.

Troop Carrier Provisions:

In the troop transport role the Globemaster could carry a maximum of 200 combat troops. To accomplish this, the main cabin was provisioned with a stowable upper deck. This upper decking was stowed into the left and right hand sides of the upper sections of the main cabin. When required the decking could be unlocked and, being hinged at the left and right sides, lowered and secured in place with stanchions. Web seating would then be installed for the troops. As an air ambulance the aircraft was designed to carry a maximum of 127 litter patents. The litters were installed in 4 rows of 5 stacked one top of the other. More on this in the next chapter.

1. Photo is a view of aircraft 42-65402. Anti-glare paint around the pilot and co-pilot blisters was added after pilots complained of the glare from the polished aluminum skin. Aircraft in background include B-17 bombers just behind the C-74. Some of the other aircraft in the distant background include B-24 bombers, A-26 attack aircraft, and C-47 transports. (Photo credits - Smithsonian)

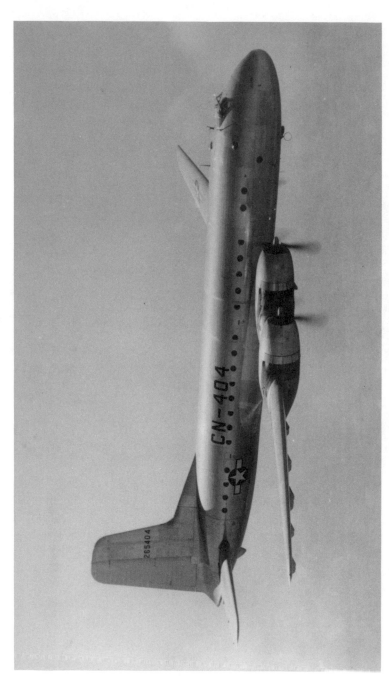

2. Photo shows aircraft 42-65404 in flight. The C-74 was actually a very aesthetic looking aircraft. The Douglas lineage, as evidenced by the clean lines and appealing design, can be seen in this photo. Note the position of the pilot and co-pilot under the two blisters. One can readily understand why pilots did not like this type of arrangement. (Photo credits - Smithsonian)

3. C-74 flight deck main instrument panel. The photo was take in June of 1945. Most notable is the dated Radio Compass Indicators located on the lower center section of the instrument panel. Lack of much engine instruments was typical of the Globemaster I and II. Also shown in the photo is an unusual flight control wheel arrangement between the pilot and co-pilot. The pilots control wheel appears to be instrumented in some manner, while the co-pilots wheel is more typical of the era, and appears to be a production wheel with the Douglas name and logo on the center hub. Blisters are evident above the pilot and co-pilot. (Photo credits - Douglas)

4 Photo shows a jeep being loaded into a C-74 via the amidships loading platform. Visible to the left and right of the opening under the aircraft are the two hydraulically operated cargo loading doors, as well as the loading ramp cabling. Main landing gear tires in the foreground are each approximately five feet in diameter. Aircraft in background are B-17 bombers with engines removed. (Photo credits - Smithsonian)

5. Photo shows aircraft 42-65402, the first C-74 manufactured. Volume of square footage for loading through the open forward cargo door is evident by comparing the three individuals standing in the open door area. Hoisting crane is positioned in the forward portion of the door opening and was used to hoist cargo into the aircraft. Based on the activity taking place around this aircraft, and the jeep parked on the ramp inboard of the number two engine, it appears as though the ground crew is preparing to hoist the jeep into the aircraft. (Photo credits - Smithsonian)

Chapter II
EVOLUTION: GLOBEMASTER II

The C-74 design evolved into what became the Douglas Model 1129A, later redesignated by the USAF as the C-124. In February of 1949, work started on converting the fifth production C-74 (serial number 42-65406) into the YC-124A prototype. The redesigned aircraft retained the same wing and tail surfaces as the C-74. However, an additional 3 feet was added to the fuselage length, and an upper deck was added increasing the overall height by 5 feet. Ground clearance under the nose was reduced by 6 feet. The odd looking blister canopies were replaced with conventional transport type windscreens and flight deck. Pilots did not appreciate the blister canopies as they restricted the visibility and field of view of both pilots. The gross weight grew from 145,000 pounds for the C-74 to 175,000 pounds for the prototype C-124. This weight increase made the C-124 two and one half times heavier than the then in use Douglas C-54 Skymaster (the civilian DC-4). The fuselage was revised to add a double decked main cabin, and a set of nose loading clamshell doors were incorporated into the fuselage. The C-124A's top speed was 298 mph, with a cruise speed of 265 mph, with a 25 ton payload. The aircraft could fly 2,300 miles and had a maximum unrefueled range of 6,280 miles. The first flight of the YC-124, (the "Y" designation indicates the aircraft is a prototype), took place on November 27, 1949. The new aircraft was assigned to Edwards Air Force Base on April 21, 1950 for flight test. A very successful flight test program was concluded in August of 1950. A total of two prototypes were built for flight test, and eventually the "Y" designation was dropped and the two aircraft officially became C-124's. The first delivery of the production aircraft, the C-124A took place in May 1950, with a total of 204 "A" models built. The "A" version differed slightly from the basic C-124 model in that the C-124 had Pratt & Whitney R-4360-20 engines producing 3,000 horse power each. The C-124A had the modified R-4360-35 engines which produced 3,500 horse power each. The prototype and production aircraft had a flight deck featuring pilots seated side by side, with dual flight controls and instrumentation. Aft of the pilot, on the left side of the flight deck were positions for the navigator and the radio operator. The flight deck also contained a small galley and a crew rest area with small beds. Housed in the ceiling of the flight deck was a Plexiglas bubble that the navigator would stand under with a sextant and "shoot the stars." Using readings from the sextant the navigator would then plot the aircraft position as the flight progressed. The age of Inertial Navigation Systems and Ground Positioning Systems was far into the future. A flight engineer was seated behind the co-pilot. There were two versions of the flight engineers position. One version seated the engineer aft of the co-pilot, facing forward. The second version, established as the final configuration, placed the engineer aft of the co-pilot facing right, with the instrument panel on the right hand side of the flight deck. This version placed the instrument panel in such a position as to allow the pilot to view the engine instruments if required.

To gain entry into the aircraft the aircrew normally entered through a small access door built into the lower section of the right hand clamshell door, just forward of the nose landing gear. Once the access door was opened, a self-contained a built-in boarding ladder could be extended to gain entry. In the main cargo compartment another ladder climb was required up to the flight deck. This ladder closely resembled a painter's ladder, leaning at an angle and bolted to the main cabin floor at one end, and to the flight deck entranceway on the other end. The ladder was extremely difficult and dangerous to climb during turbulent weather.

Everything about this aircraft was huge. The wingspan measured 174 feet, 2 inches; it had a length of 130 feet, and a height of 48 feet, 3 inches. The cargo hold had a length of 77 feet, a height of 12 feet, 10 inches and a width of 13 feet. The usable cargo space was some 10,000 cubic feet. The nose of the aircraft opened via a set of clamshell doors. With the doors open an area 11 feet 8 inches by 11 feet 4 inches was exposed. Built into the nose of the aircraft were two loading ramps. Each ramp was hinged at its mid point, and would fold in two for stowage with the doors closed. With the doors open the ramps could be extended. Quite a wide variety of tracked and wheeled vehicles could be driven into or off the aircraft.

In addition to loading cargo through the nose clamshell doors, an electrically operated loading platform was also available. This device was built into the cabin floor amidships, just aft of the wing trailing edges. The loading platform was held in place via a set of locking devices, and when not in use actually made up a portion of the cabin flooring. To load cargo, a set of external doors would be hydraulically opened on the underside of the aircraft. Two overhead traveling cranes, that ran the length of the cabin, were used to lower and raise the loading platform. These cranes were capable of lifting up to 16,000 pounds. The traveling cranes were also used to transfer cargo within the cabin area. Cargo aircraft of this era did not contain cargo rollers built into the flooring to allow easy movement of material within the aircraft as are incorporated into modern cargo aircraft. As can be seen, some extensive thinking on the part of Douglas Aircraft went into the cargo handling design of this aircraft.

Diversification was also a key factor built into the design of the aircraft, as it was capable of carrying 200 fully equipped combat troops in an unusual stowable upper deck. The deck was built in two hinged pieces, with the hinges built into the aircraft longerons, on the left and right hand sides of the cabin. When in use, the decks would swing down, and be supported on several legs. The cabin could then be configured to carry 200 fully equipped combat troops. It was also designed to carry 94 percent of all military vehicles, fully assembled, in use at the time. When used as an air ambulance, it could carry 127 litter patients and the necessary doctors and nurses required to attend to the patients.

One of the more unusual features of the aircraft was the fact that maintenance could be performed on the engines while in flight. The flight engineer could climb down into a compartment under the main cabin flooring, open a small circular door, and climb out into a crawlway in the forward section of the wing. This crawlway lead to the backside of each engine, the engine firewall. Attached to the firewall was a small door that could be lowered. This door allowed access to the rear of the engine, and a wide variety of components that could be replaced. In-flight maintenance is covered in detail later in this chapter. Suffice it to say that performing maintenance on the engines while in flight was only done during emergencies. Maintenance under these condition was dangerous, hot, noisy, and time consuming. Consider for a moment climbing out into a crawlway just large enough for a normal sized person to squeeze through on hands and knees. Then, if access to the inboard engines was required, climbing over the main landing gear, to reach the engine firewall door. The engine would of course be shut down and the propeller feathered, but the sounds of the outboard engine as well as the rush of air over the wing and through the cracks in the gear doors would be deafening. Once the door was lowered, considerable heat would radiate from the engine. If a component required replacement it would be hot and difficult to handle in the small confines. These type tasks were considered a normal duty for a Globemaster flight engineer.

On March 2, 1951, the Military Air Transport Service (MATS) established the C-124 Heavy Transition Training Unit (HTTU) at McChord Air Force Base in Washington state. The mission of the C-124 HTTU was the training of all flight crews and ground personnel in the safe and efficient operation of the C-124 aircraft. The HTTU was also known as the 1740th Air Transport Squadron. The HTTU reviewed course of instruction on maintenance and operations at Walker Air Force Base, New Mexico, and observed the operation of the C-74. These reviews and observations turned out to be beneficial in the field of engine conditioning and hydraulic systems operation and maintenance.

During February of 1952, a conference was held to determine what, if any, items of equipment could be removed from the C-124 to provide for an increase in payload lift and delivery range. The conference conducted studies involving removal of items, and corresponding weight values gained. The studies revealed that removal of items of equipment looked into was not justified in the interest of maintaining the versatility of the aircraft. The conference concluded that based on studies accomplished no justification could be made to alter the aircraft's standard equipment package. One of the more interesting items looked into was the potential for removing the nose loading ramps. Each ramp weighed 942 pounds, which did not include the weight of the cabling system and hydraulic system required to operate the ramps. In all, removal of the ramps could have potentially shaved approximately 2,000 pounds from the aircraft's basic weight. The drawbacks were the aft movement of the center of gravity, and as the study concluded, a reduction in aircraft versatility.

The International Geophysical Year of 1957-1958 was supported in part with Globemaster II flights to Antarctica as part of Operation Deep Freeze. The aircraft and support structure were assigned as members of Task Force 43. Flights from the continental U.S. to Antarctica would usually start from Travis AFB, CA. First stop on the trip was Hickam AFB, Hawaii, then onto the Fiji Islands, Melbourne Australia and finally to Christ Church, New Zealand. From this rear area staging base, the aircraft would fly to Williams Air Operating Facility at McMurdo Sound in Antarctica. McMurdo was considered a forward staging area, and from this location the Globemaster's would, if required, fly onto base camps at or near the South Pole to air drop supplies to the teams of scientist and technicians assigned to the camps. These air drops were accomplished by lifting the loading platform out of the main cabin floor, opening the lower cargo loading doors and dropping the cargo through the opening. As can be expected, the aircraft became extremely cold inside during these operations. Navigation was an ever present problem and hazard with flights near the poles, as the magnetic compass and electronic navigation equipment onboard were unreliable due to the magnetic field of the earth at the poles. Two navigators were always assigned on these flights, and they would navigate by the use of the old reliable sextant, and dead reckoning.

During the early 1960's C-124's performed a unique role in supporting our fledgling manned space flight program. The aircraft were routinely flown to the McDonnell Aircraft factory located at Lambert Field in St. Louis. From this facility the Mercury and Gemini capsules would be loaded onto the aircraft through the nose loading doors. The capsules would then be flown to Cape Canaveral, Florida for operational checkout and then mating to their boosters for the trip into space. The reason for transport on the Globemaster was simple, size. The Mercury Spacecraft, for example, was 7 feet 3 inches long, 6 feet, 2 ½ inches in diameter, and weighed 2,422 pounds for shipping. The craft was mounted on a transportation trailer, which in itself was also very large and heavy. The aircraft also transported Thor ICBM's to England starting in 1959 through 1961. The Globemaster was the only aircraft capable of transporting these large ICBM's during this time frame.

The final production version of the Globemaster II was designated as the Douglas Model 1317, the C-124C. The "C" model empty weight was 101,000 pounds and had a normal gross weight of 185,000 pounds. The aircraft performance manual did allow for a gross take-of weight of up to 200,500 pounds under certain conditions. The "C" version could carry a 50,000 pound load 1,000 statute miles, and return to base without refueling. An alternate gross take-off weight of 194,500 pounds allowed the aircraft to fly 2,300 statute miles carrying a 50,000 pound payload. The payload could be increased to more than 70,000 pounds by reducing the range to destination. The engines were upgraded to the R-4360-63 configuration resulting in a horsepower output of 3,800 per engine.

The "C" version was fitted with an APS-42 search radar system (mounted in the very evident nose radome). This was a weather radar that was the predecessor to the type of weather radar found on most modern commercial and military transports. The 1703rd Air Transport Group at Brookley Air Force Base Alabama became the first operational unit to receive the new "C" model.

The improvements incorporated into the "C" model were later retrofitted into the C-124A. The USAF issued several modifications upgrading the "A"s to "C" models. Onc of the major modifications included replacement of the R4360-20WA engines with the R4360-63A. Visual changes to the aircraft included the installation of the APS-42 search radar and radome. Completion of all of the modifications resulted in the USAF issuing Technical Order 1C-124A-550, which redesignated the C-124A to the C-124C, thereby standardizing the aircraft designation. Although the "A" model designation was changed, the standardization did not cover some aircraft systems. As an example, the wing trailing edge flaps on some models was of the original full span flap configuration used in the C-74. The "C" was being manufactured with partial span trailing edge flaps. Wingtip heaters were also an item that the "C" model was manufactured with that converted "A"s did not have incorporated. The production "C" was manufactured with a 12 tank fuel system, "A"s that were converted to "C"s retained the older 6 tank fuel system. Appendix II provides a basic difference listing of C-124A's that were converted to "C"s and the differences between these aircraft.

The last Globemaster II was delivered to the USAF on May 9, 1955. In June of 1970 the Globemaster II fleet completed a milestone by passing 150,000 flight hours accident free. The last of the Globemaster II's were phased out of Air National Guard and Air Force Reserve units in 1974 due to safety of flight concerns centered on extensive corrosion discovered in the outer wing panels. This problem surfaced initially with the crash of C-124C serial number 52-1075 over Cordova, Maryland. The right hand wing separated outboard of the number 4 engine. This crash led to airspeed and envelope restrictions being place on the aircraft. During its five year production run a total of 449 C-124's were built at the Douglas facility in Long Beach California. See Appendix II for a complete listing of the Globemaster II's production run. The YC-124 prototype (C-74 conversion) was flown by a MATS unit at Kelly Air Force Base in Texas until the early 1960's. Upon retirement from service it was flown to Fairborn Air Force Base, Ohio and placed on display. The aircraft remained on display at Fairborn for several years, and was finally scrapped when the base closed.

Operational Losses:

Approximately 40 aircraft had sustained Class A mishaps during the operational lifetime of the Globemaster II. A Class A mishap is one in which the aircraft sustains damages in excess of one million dollars, or loss of life has resulted from the mishap. Thirteen of these mishaps were directly related to engine problems. Three of the mishap aircraft successfully ditched at sea, quite a feat for such a large aircraft with clamshell doors in the nose. The Appendix section at the end of this book provides a listing of Globemaster II Class A mishaps. One in-flight incident that did not result in the loss of life or aircraft, but could have had grave consequences, took place in 1953. Mid summer of 1953 cadets of the Air Force Reserve Officers Training Corps experienced a once in a lifetime event during a training flight over Texas. The 200 cadets on board were ordered to bail out of a stricken Globemaster II. Fortunately after the mass bailout the pilots were able make a successful emergency landing.

C-124's in the Movies:

Unlike other USAF transport aircraft, the C-124 was camera shy. One of the very few Hollywood movies made with the C-124 in it was Paramont Pictures "Strategic Air Command," starring Jimmy Stewart and June Allyson. Approximately half way through this great 1955 movie, several C-124A's can be seen loading cargo and passenger's for an overseas deployment (or so the script went) to Japan. The movie did show some of the unusual features of the aircraft.

There are scenes showing the opening of the nose clamshell doors, and the loading ramps being extended. Another shows the aircraft loading platform on the ramp under the aircraft, with cargo being loaded onto it. A fuel truck being driven into one of the aircraft is also shown, and provides graphic evidence of the volume available within the main cargo compartment. What appears to be a spare R4360 engine being loaded into the aircraft is also shown. The engine loading provides a scaled view of just how large the engine is when compared to the several technicians that are standing next to it. The movie also provides the viewer a look at some early Military Air Transport Squadron paint schemes. The final scene of a Globemaster in the movie shows one aircraft taxing out of its parking spot. This scene clearly shows the scanner stationed in the opened navigators bubble observing the exterior of the aircraft for clearance and safety.

Globemaster's in Museums:

Only eight C-124's are on display at Air Museums. The following is a listing of these aircraft:

The McChord AFB Air Museum in Washington state has on display C-124C serial number 52-0994. In October of 1986 this aircraft was flown from Selfridge Air National Guard Base in Michigan to McChord AFB to become part of the McChord Museum.

The Travis Air Force Base Museum, located near Fairfield, California has on display C-124C serial number 50-2100. This aircraft was discovered at the Aberdeen Proving Grounds, made flight worthy by a volunteer force and flown to Dover AFB, Delaware for servicing and inspection. It was subsequently flown to Dobbins AFB in Georgia for further inspections and partial refurbishment again by a volunteer crew. Its final flight was from Dobbins to Travis to be inducted into the Travis Air Base Museum. The restoration crew at Travis has done an outstanding job of putting this aircraft back into almost mint condition, and is a must to see for any aviation buff.

The Pima County Air Museum, located near Tucson, Arizona possesses C-124C Globemaster II, serial number 52-1004. The aircraft was delivered to the museum in 1975, and has had quite a history. Delivered to the USAF in November of 1953, it served until December of 1973, when it was dropped from the USAF inventory. It has served at Brookely AFB in Alabama; Norton AFB in California; Palm Beach AFB in Florida; Dover AFB Delaware, and Hickam AFB in Hawaii. With the Air Force Reserves, it conducted missions from Barksdale AFB, and Greater Pittsburgh Air Base.

The Wright Patterson Air Force Base Museum in Dayton Ohio possesses a C-124C serial number 52-1066. As with all aircraft on display at this Air Force Museum, the aircraft is in outstanding condition. This particular aircraft was in operational service from 1950 to 1974 and was apparently one of the very last aircraft in operation service.

The Hill Air Force Base Museum in Utah is the proud owner of C-124C serial number 53-0050. This aircraft was one of two discovered at the Aberdeen Proving Grounds in Maryland, made flight worthy by a volunteer force and flown to Dover AFB, Delaware for servicing and inspection. It was the subsequently flown to Dobbins AFB in Georgia for further inspections and partial refurbishment again by a volunteer crew. Its final flight was from Dobbins to Hill to be inducted into the Hill Air Base Museum.

The Strategic Air Command (SAC) Museum at Offut Air Force Base, Nebraska has C-124A serial number 49-0258 on display outdoors. This aircraft was assigned to SAC from 1950 until 1961. This particular aircraft not only served with SAC, but also with the Military Air Transport Service (MATS) as well as the U.S.A.F. Reserves. The aircraft flew troops and cargo from assignments in Oklahoma, Hawaii, Japan, and Texas. This aircraft came to the SAC Museum from the 916th Military Airlift Group (USAF Reserves), Carswell AFB, Texas.

The Charleston Air Force Base Museum at Charleston, South Carolina's outdoor display of C-124C serial number 52-1072 is a must see. The aircraft is in good shape, and served with the U.S.A.F. Reserves prior to being placed on permanent display at the museum.

Finally, the only C-124 on display outside of the U.S. is at the Korean Military Academy Museum. This C-124C, serial number 52-0943 was donated to the museum by the USAF.

Summary of Selected Aircraft Systems

Cargo Loading

Nose Loading System - The aircraft was equipped with two hydraulically operated clamshell type nose loading doors. In the closed position the doors formed the lower forward section of the aircraft outer moldline. Vertical clearance through the open doors was 11 feet 7 inches, lateral clearance was 11 feet 3 inches. Also contained within the aircraft immediately aft of the clamshell doors were two hydraulically operated loading ramps. For outsized cargo loading, such as tanks, trucks, or other tracked/wheeled vehicles, the clamshell doors would be opened by hydraulic pressure from an electrically driven hydraulic pump. The doors could also be opened manually by the use of a hand pump. A control panel to operate the doors and ramps were readily accessible within the aircraft near the doors. Once the clamshell doors were open, the loading ramps could be hydraulically lowered using pressure from the same hydraulic pump used to open the doors. The clamshell doors were extremely rugged and could be operated in winds up to 43 knots from any direction. The width between the two loading ramps could be adjusted to allow for the loading of a wide variety of vehicles onto the aircraft. The hydraulic actuator used to operate the doors was, and may still be, the longest hydraulic actuator ever installed on an aircraft. In the event of a ground emergency the nose loading doors could be manually jettisoned to allow for near immediate exit from the aircraft.

The nose loading ramps were each 36 inches wide. They could be positioned from a minimum of 24 inches apart, to a maximum of 50 inches apart. The ramps were placed 50 inches apart when stowed in the up position. Maximum loading on each ramp was 25,000 pounds, for a total ramp weight of 50,000 pounds. Each ramp weighed 942 pounds, and as stated previously, were hydraulically operated from a control panel within the aircraft.

Loading Platform System - The aircraft was also equipped with a loading platform that formed a section of the main cabin floor. The platform was raised and lowered by electrically driven traveling cranes. This loading method was carried over from the C-74 Globemaster I. When the platform was not in use, it was enclosed within the aircraft by two hydraulically operated cargo doors on the underside of the external section of the aircraft. The external doors could also be operated manually by using an emergency hydraulic hand pump located within the main cabin of the aircraft. When the platform was required for use, the external cargo loading doors on the underside of the aircraft would be hydraulically opened, and steel cables from the electrically operated overhead traveling cranes would be attached to the platform. The platform could then be unlocked from the main cabin floor and lower to the ground via the overhead cranes. Cargo would then be placed on the platform which would then be raised back into the aircraft. Once in the aircraft the loaded platform could be moved forward or aft within the main cabin, which aided in the unloading or movement of cargo within the aircraft. When both electrically operated cranes were used together for cargo loading operations, a maximum load of 16,000 pounds could be hoisted into or out of the aircraft. The loading platform could be jettisoned in flight if required. The electrically operated overhead traveling cranes could also be operated manually in an emergency. Hand cranks would be attached to the ends of the electric motors and the cranes could be manually cranked to raise or lower the loading platform.

Overhead Traveling Cranes - The two overhead cranes, or hoists, were electrically operated, and independently controlled. A cargo hoist master switch controlled power for both hoists. Each hoist weighted 385.5 pounds, operated at 2.86 horsepower drawing 185 amps. The operational limit of the hoists was 3 minutes on and 2 minutes off. To operate the hoists in the manual (emergency) mode, a hand-crank gear was provided with a ratio of 112 to 1. The hoists traveled on a rail system that stretched 564 inches overhead, down the length of the main cabin. The hoist cables were ¼ inch in diameter, with a usable length of 50 feet. The traversing power units for the electrical hoists allowed for hoist travel within the main cabin at a rate of 55 to 65 feet per minute.

Airdrop Provisions

Globemaster II's were provisioned to airdrop a maximum of 112 paratroopers or up to twenty A-22 cargo containers, or a combination of both. Paratroops departed the aircraft via the aft cabin exit doors. Four static line anchor cables, one for each row of troop seats, were provided for the attachment of static lines. The cables were arranged in two pairs, one pair on either side of the fuselage centerline, and extended between two anchor cable supports. Cargo was dropped through the platform well or ejected through the aft cabin exit doors.

Cargo Jettisoning

During emergencies, such as when one or more engines are inoperative, procedures could have called for the jettisoning of cargo in-flight. During such event, the aircraft was slowed to 130 KIAS (Knots Indicated Air Speed). Airspeeds higher than this may have allowed the cargo to strike the underside of the aircraft as it exited. The cabin ventilating air and heat valves were closed, which prevented buffeting. Normally the loading platform was not jettisoned as retaining it provided a safe walkway after the cargo was jettisoned. Personnel would then don retaining harnesses, and jettison cargo out of the open loading well. The overhead cranes could be used in conjunction with the loading platform to move cargo within the main cabin and the open loading well. Teamwork was required during this operation, as the potential for large changes in the aircraft center of gravity could take place. Communication between the pilot and loadmaster was essential, as large changes in aircraft pitch associated with cargo movement/jettison could take place. Due to the boundary layer flow around the aircraft, light cargo sometimes would not exit the open well. The recommended procedure for light cargo was to close the lower cargo doors (external doors), fill the well with the light cargo, then open the doors. Once all the required cargo was removed from the aircraft, the lower doors were closed, and if retained, the loading platform would then be secured in place.

Flight Control System:

Compared to modern transport aircraft, the C-124 flight control system was rudimentary. The primary system consisted of a set of ailerons, elevators, and a rudder. The elevators and rudder incorporated an aerodynamic boost to reduce the amount of force the pilot was required to exert on the control yoke to move a control surface. A combination trim and servo tab was provided on the rudder, with separate trim tabs and servo tabs on the elevators. The ailerons were mechanically linked to the control stick, however there was an independent hydraulic boost system incorporated.

Most of the C-124's built were delivered with ailerons that automatically moved with the flaps to aid in lift at low speed, part of the "full span flap" configuration. On later aircraft the wing flaps were of the partial span type, which did not incorporate aileron movement with flap setting. The conversion from full span to partial span flaps was a trade off in performance verses reduced weight and cost with an increase in reliability. Witness the following example: At 180,000 pounds, with a flap deflection of 20 degrees a full span flap aircraft would have and approach speed of 135 knots, while a partial span flap aircraft's approach speed would be 137 knots. With the same weight and flap deflections, the full span flap aircraft would have a threshold speed of 125 knots, a partial span aircraft's threshold speed would be 126 knots. Power off stall speed is also different between these aircraft, for example: with a gross weight of 180,000 pounds, again with 20 degrees flap deflection, the full span flap aircraft had an unaccellerated flight stall speed of 104 knots, while the part span aircraft's unaccellerated stall speed was 105 knots. The full span flap aircraft did have one performance increase that the part span aircraft did not, and that was an additional 200 feet per minute increase in 3 engine climb performance.

The Linked Tab System was a system in common use at the time. The elevator and rudder used this system on all C-124's. The system effectively divided the pilots input force between the primary control surface and a servo tab. With this system, the servo tab deflects and aerodynamic force acting on the tab aided in moving the control surface. The end result of this system was to lower the forces required by the pilot moving the control yoke to reposition a control surface.

The flight control system contained the standard rudder, elevator, and aileron trim system. The aileron trim system was electrically operated by an actuator located in the right aileron. The actuator was controlled by a switch located on the left side of the pilots control pedestal. The system operated only the right aileron trim tab, the left being in a fixed position, (although it could be mechanically adjusted on the ground if required). An aileron tab position indicator was located on the pilots main instrument panel. Both the actuator and the indicator operated off of the aircraft's 28 volt DC power system.

The rudder and elevator trim systems were both operated mechanically. The pilot would operate a control wheel for either system, which would in turn mechanically reposition the control surfaces. Rudder and elevator position indicators were marked directly onto the control wheels. One novel feature of the flight control system were the control surface snubber's. With the huge size of the ailerons, rudder, and elevators on the aircraft, wind gusts acting on these surfaces would toss the control wheel and rudder pedals creating problems for the pilot. When engaged, the snubber's would lock the control surfaces, thus assisting the pilot in taxiing when wind gust loads made control of the aileron rudder and elevator surfaces difficult. They also kept the controls from buffeting when the aircraft was parked.

Fuel System:

As with the Globemaster I, all of the fuel carried in the Globemaster II was carried in the wings only. The fuel system on the C-124 varied with the year and lot the aircraft was built in. Initially, the fuel system was a carry over from the C-74. However as the years progressed, the system was upgraded from a totally mechanical system to a somewhat electrical system, as per these examples:

Refueling - Fuel servicing took place in one of two methods, depending on the aircraft serial number range.

Serial Numbers 49-243 through 50-1268 - Fuel was carried in two outboard wing tanks, two inboard wing tanks, and two auxiliary wing tanks, for a total of 6 wing tanks. Fully serviced aircraft within this serial number range carried 11,000 gallons of grade 115/145 gasoline, which is equivalent to about 66,000 pounds. Aircraft within this serial number range were refueled "over-the-wing", which meant that each fuel tank required servicing individually. This was a carry over from the Globemaster I. On the Globemaster II, this meant that the person performing the refueling on top of the wing was 13 feet above the ground.

Serial Numbers 49-251 through 51-132 - Fuel was carried in the same arrangement as the above serial number range (49-243 through 50-1286). However, although the total fuel carried was the same, the amount of usable fuel was slightly reduced. This was due to a slight reduction in total useful carried in the wing outboard and inboard fuel tanks. Some of the aircraft within this block (serial numbers 51-73 and subsequent) were equipped with the single point refueling system (see below).

Serial Numbers 51-73 and Subsequent - These aircraft incorporated the "single-point" refueling system. The method cut servicing time down significantly. The flight engineer or mechanic simply connected the refueling hose up to a receptacle under the aircraft at the centerline, which was just forward of the aircraft main landing gear. A refueling control panel, located just aft of the refueling receptacle, allowed the flight engineer or mechanic control over the distribution of fuel within the aircraft as well as testing the refuel system for proper operation. When the aircraft was fully serviced, the fuel flow automatically stopped.

Serial Numbers 51-132 and subsequent - The fuel system on aircraft starting with 51-132 was radically redesigned. Aircraft built starting with serial number 51-132 were equipped with a 12 tank wing fuel system. Total fuel carried on these aircraft grew to 11,216 gallons equivalent to 67,298 pounds of grade 115/145 gasoline.

In-flight Operations - Control of the fuel system in-flight was the responsibility of the flight engineer. The engineers control table and station was significantly different between aircraft, per the following examples:

Serial Numbers 49-243 through 51-132 - The flight engineers station's control table contained six mechanically operated fuel tank selector levers. These levers were mechanically connected to corresponding fuel tank control valves. This design was carried over from the C-74. When a lever was pulled aft, a mechanical steel cable linkage and pulley system pulled the fuel tank control valve to the off position. Conversely, pushing the lever forward opened the valve.

Serial Numbers 51-133 through 51-5197 - Starting with this block of aircraft, control of the fuel system changed from a strictly mechanical system to an electric system. Aircraft within this serial number range had an electrical fuel system control panel mounted on the left hand side of the flight engineers control table. The positive control operation of fuel tank valves with the mechanical system was sacrificed for the simplicity and maintainability of the electrical system. Now with the flick of a switch, the fuel valves could be opened and closed as required by the engineer. This is the same basic type of system that is used on all modern commercial aircraft.

Serial Numbers 51-5198 and subsequent - The electric fuel system control panel was moved from the left hand side of the flight engineers control table on previous aircraft to the flight engineers main instrument panel. Relocation of the fuel panel was required due to the 12 tank fuel system incorporated into aircraft at this serial number range.

Electrical System

DC Power Supply System - DC power (24 to 28 volt) was supplied by 4 engine driven generators (one generator installed on each engine) and 2 aircraft batteries. Emergency or backup DC power was supplied by 2 Auxiliary Power Plants (APP's) or 1 Auxiliary Power Unit (APU), depending on the aircraft serial number range. Except for the very last block of production aircraft, the C-124 carried 2 APP's. These units were located in the wing crawlway near the number 1 and 4 engines, where they could be serviced in-flight if required. The last block of production aircraft carried 1 APU, which was located in the lower "P" compartment. The APP's were actually small piston engines each driving a generator. The APU was a turbine engine driving a single generator.

The flight engineers main instrument panel contained 4 generator control switches marked ON, Off, and Reset. The engineers instrument panel also contained 4 generator warning lights which illuminated whenever the respective generator was not supplying power to the DC circuit. Additionally, the instrument panel contained 4 generator overheat temperature indicators. These indicators illuminated whenever a generator sustained a rapid rise in temperature, or a steady rise in temperature in excess of 135 degrees Centigrade.

AC Power System - AC power (single phase 115 volt) was supplied by 2 dc operated inverters, (one main and one spare). The inverters were operated by a single phase inverter switch on the flight engineers control panel. The switch was marked Main, Off, and Spare. Warning lights on the control panel illuminated whenever the inverter was not in operation. The AC systems provided electrical power to the APS-42 search radar, and the pilot/co-pilot flight instruments. A 110 volt emergency inverter was also available to power the essential flight instruments and VHF radio in the event of a complete electrical power failure on board the aircraft. An emergency battery was also available as a source of back-up power to operate the emergency inverter.

Wingtip Heaters:

Starting with aircraft 51-73, teardrop shaped pods were installed on each wingtip. The specific purpose of the pods have generated much discussion to those not familiar with the Globemaster II. In actuality, the pods contain heaters for the wing anti-icing system. On earlier model Globemaster II, the wing leading edge anti-icing system consisted of 6 wing heaters located in the wing crawlspace, on either side of the outboard engines. Outside air entered through several ports located along the wing leading edge. The air was then ducted to the wing heaters where it was heated using aviation gasoline from the wing tanks. The heated air was then routed into the wing leading edges, again through a series of ducts. Concern over the potential for fuel leaks and fires resulted in a redesign of the wing anti icing system, and starting with aircraft 51-73, a somewhat different approach was taken. The 6 anti icing heaters were replaced with two wingtip heaters (one on each wingtip). These heaters were mounted inside of aerodynamically shaped pods. Air entered through a small opening at the front of the pod, and was then heated, using aviation gasoline. The heated air was then routed to the wing leading edges through a series of ducts. The wingtip heater did induce a drag penalty. Aircraft without the wingtip heaters, early models, 49-243 through 50-1268, required 10 brake horsepower per engine less to obtain the same cruise performance of wingtip equipped aircraft.

In-flight Emergency Repairs

The Globemaster was unique in that actual in-flight repairs could be made on the aircraft engines, landing gear, etc. The repairs/procedures listed required the flight engineer to enter the wing crawlway to gain access to the defective components. This in itself was a hazardous operation, as at times the engineer was required to climb over the landing gear, which was stored in the up position. At other times it required the engineer to gain access to the engine via the firewall entry door.

Crawlway entry procedures were strictly adhered to each time access into the wing was required. To minimize risk, the pilot would ensure the landing gear handle was in the up and locked position, whenever the crawlway was occupied. A safety observer was on station in the "P" compartment, (the lower forward equipment bay). The observer would report on the condition of the crawlway occupant, and render assistance if required. The person in the crawlway would be required to maintain radio contact, via the interphone system, to the pilot and observer. Since the crawlway contained a wide variety of control cables, valves, electrical connections/wires, etc., great care was required when traversing the crawlspace. Entry into the crawlway was made with the aircraft in smooth level flight conditions, and at altitudes between 3,000 and 10,000 feet. The following is a summary of some of the unusual and dramatic repairs a flight engineer could accomplish on the aircraft while in flight.

Main Landing Gear Emergency In-Flight Extension - In the event one or more main landing gear would not extend, an excursion into the wing crawlway would be required. After adhering to all of the safety requirements listed previously, the flight engineer/scanner would enter the crawlway via a small oval hatch and climb out into the wing. This was one of the most hazardous tasks performed on the aircraft while in-flight. Extending the left main landing gear required the engineer/scanner to climb out to the gear, and using a jamb latch wrench, apply pressure to a toggle link to unlock the gear, which in turn unlocked and fell into the airstream to the down and locked position.

As can be expected performing this operation in-flight could be hair raising. However, extending the right hand main landing gear was even more of a problem as well as a hazard. This required the engineer/scanner to climb passed the up and locked landing gear. Once on the other side of the gear, pressure would be placed on the toggle link to unlock the gear. The dilemma then facing the engineer was being on the wrong side of an extremely large opening. Normal procedure would be to remain in the crawlway until after landing and coming to a complete stop.

Engine Problems - Access to the engine while in-flight was another very hazardous operation to perform. The flight engineer would shut down and feather the problem engine. Once the engine was shut down and the prop feathered, the engineer/scanner would enter the crawlway, adhering to all of the previously stated safety requirements, and climb out to the problem engine. For the inboard engines, this required the flight engineer/scanner to climb over the top of the main landing gear, which would be in the up and locked position. Once at the engine, he could then unlock and lower the firewall access door. If the problem was associated with a fuel pressure drop, the engineer could potentially be exposed to fuel spray or vapors.

A generator failure would require the engineer/scanner to lower the firewall access door to inspect the generator for an overheat condition. If evidence of an overhear condition existed, the generator could be replaced in-flight. Manually operating the engine oil cooler doors and cowl flaps also required access to the engine via the firewall access door. Once the firewall door had been lowered, the oil cooler doors or cowl flaps could be hand cranked to the desired position.

C-124 CIVILIAN AIRLIFT OPERATIONS:

A history of the C-124 would not be complete without commenting on the humanitarian flights that the Globemaster II provided to the world during its years with the Military Air Transport Service. Starting in 1953 and ending in 1970 the aircraft flew to the four corners of the globe providing supplies and at times removing personnel from harms way. These then are some of the most notable efforts:

1953 - Just three years after the first flight of the prototype YC-124, a production Globemaster II participated in Operation "Big Switch." The end of the Korean War brought the exchange of prisoners of war, and the Military Air Transport Service

(MATS) provided the aircraft to fly our POW's home after confinement in North Korea. The MATS aircraft included in this operation were C-46's, C-47's, C-54's, C-97's as well as the C-124.

1954 - Devastating floods ravaged India and Pakistan in August of 1954. Working through the U. S. State Department, the USAF provided approximately 27 cargo planes to transport over 150 tons of supplies to the stricken regions of both countries. C-124's were part of this effort, transporting needed medical supplies, food, clothing, etc.

1955 - The French Indochina colonial empire fell in 1955 after a long war that unfortunately would be repeated a mere decade later. Five C-124's along with C-97's and C-118's (a total of 20 aircraft) provided evacuation flights for 504 wounded soldiers from Indochina back to France. In October of this year, C-124's delivered fire fighting equipment in an effort to assist the Japanese control a major oil storage fire.

1955 - The island of Iwo Jima was devastated by a typhoon. The USAF dispatched 7 C-124's to fly in radio equipment, generators, beacons, a complete airport control tower, tents, and supplies. This was required as all buildings on the island were destroyed.

1959 - In September C-124's airlifted relief supplies to Nagoya, Japan. The city was severely hit by a typhoon.

1960 - March 1960 C-124's were required to respond to flooding in Brazil. Six Globemaster's airlifted two rescue helicopters and 160 tons of supplies. In May a devastating series of earthquakes racked Chile, some of which registered seven on the Richter scale. The earthquakes set off a series of tidal waves, landslides, and avalanches. Initial reports indicated approximately 8,000 persons were dead with 5,500 injured. Somewhere near 240,00 people were left homeless. The U.S. State Department again responded tasking the U.S. Air Force with humanitarian relief. Operation "Amigos Airlift" was started and the C-124 was again called into service to supply the people of Chile with life's basic necessities. During this year Pakistan experienced the wrath of nature again when a cyclone struck East Pakistan in mid 1960. The USAF responded by sending seven C-124's and C-130's. These 7 aircraft carried a total of 89 tons of supplies to the people of East Pakistan.

1960 - During October, Globemaster's, primarily from the 436th Airlift Wing, participated in "Operation New Tape". This operation was in response to a United Nations request for assistance in support of UN efforts in the Congo Republic. The 436th provided 28 aircraft and 37 aircrews much of the effort being provided by C-124 aircraft and crews. The operation lasted into 1964, and C-124 aircrews were instrumental in providing supplies into the Congo Republic as well as flying refugee's out of harms way.

1961 - In October the USAF conducted relief efforts into Cambodia. Two C-130's and seven C-124's transported approximately 260 tons of construction equipment and needed supplies to assist the Cambodian government cope with the aftermath of floods that brought death and destruction to the country.

1962 - The Iranian earthquake of 1962 required the support of 47 planes delivering 900 tons of cargo. This same year the island of Guam was struck by a typhoon requiring additional humanitarian flights. Fifty cargo planes delivered approximately 970 tons of supplies to the island, and aided in the evacuation of over 760 persons. C-124's proved key in the humanitarian efforts during the year.

1963 - February brought severe snow to the Korean peninsula. Globemaster's flew in mail and food to a Korean island stranded by the severe weather. This same year, Hurricane Flora extensively damaged the infrastructure of Tobago. A single C-124 delivered 385 tents and cots in an effort to provide some comfort to displaced citizens.

1964 - A significant year for relief efforts. In June the eastern section of Brazil sustained heavy rains and subsequent flooding. Two C-124's airlifted 120 tons of supplies to the citizens of that country. Floods ravaged South Vietnam during the latter part of 1964. The USAF responded by sending C-124's as well as other cargo aircraft. More than 2,000 tons of supplies were delivered and approximately 1,500 citizens were evacuated from the flooded areas. Also during this year C-124's participated in Operation "Helping Hand", providing earthquake victims in Anchorage, Alaska with medical supplies, clothing, boats, etc. In August Hurricane Cleo struck Guadeloupe and a single C-124 delivered 7 tons of relief supplies. In October, ten Globemaster's delivered approximately 160 tons of supplies to aid the citizens of Yugoslavia in relief from problems associated with a natural disaster.

1966 - In February of this year a hurricane struck the Samoan Islands. Three C-124's were dispatched to Pago Pago with electrical power generating equipment, food, and construction material. October of this same year saw Globemaster's delivering tents, food, and supplies to the Dominican Republic, after a hurricane had devastated the island.

1969 - In response to the devastation of the Gulf Coast caused by Hurricane Camille, C-124's as well as C-119's transported 339 passengers and 1,259 tons of cargo to the devastated areas, primarily in Mississippi.

1970 - In May three C-124's carried 16 tons of supplies to Puerto Rico in an effort to provide aid to the citizens after a hurricane devastated the island.

A FLIGHT ACROSS THE POND:

In the early 1970's, the 336th Military Airlift Squadron, of the 452nd Military Airlift Wing operated out of Hamilton Air Force Base California. The base was located near the small town of Navato, just north of San Francisco. The 336th was one of the very few units in the Air Force Reserves still operating the C-124. All regular Air Force C-124 units had either been deactivated or had transitioned to the Lockheed C-141 Starlifter or C-130 Hercules. The decision to retain a few C-124 units in the Air Force Reserve was made based on the need to carry cargo of unusually large dimensions that would not fit into the C-141or C-130. The aircraft would remain in service until sufficient quantities of Lockheed C-5A Galaxy transports became operational, and the service's felt sufficient airlift capabilities existed as more C-141's and upgraded C-130's entered service.

The squadron operated the C-124C version of the Globemaster II. One would expect an aircraft that had been in service for twenty years would have a standard configuration established. However, the configuration varied between assigned aircraft. For example, the flight engineers station on some aircraft was positioned behind the co-pilot with the flight engineer facing forward. A second configuration placed the flight engineer behind the co-pilot, facing sideways toward the right hand side of the flight deck. One other notable aircraft difference was the fact that the several of the aircraft were not configured with single point refueling. These aircraft had to be fueled "over the wing". As stated previously in this book, this method of refueling was a carry-over from the original C-74

Globemaster I. To refuel the aircraft, a technician would be required to gain access to the top of the wing through the main cabin. Once on top of the wing, the fuel hose would be passed up to him, and after the wing fuel caps were opened, fuel would be pumped into the six individual wing tanks. As can be expected, this took quite a long time, as the aircraft held 11,000 gallons. All other aircraft were refueled via a single point refueling receptacle mounted in an access panel on the underside of the airplane centerline, just forward of the main landing gear.

As stated in the introduction to this book, the C-124 was considered the last of the "flight engineers' airplanes." The following scenario would be considered typical duties for a flight engineer on a Globemaster II mission from California to Southeast Asia and return during the early 1970's.

ONE DAY PRIOR TO THE TRIP:

Two flight engineers were required on each flight. One engineer acted as the "panel operator," operating and monitoring the engine, fuel, and associated controls during flight. The second engineer acted as what was called a "scanner," remaining in the main cabin, observing the engines and inspecting the aircraft during flight. If the flight was of a significantly long duration, the two engineers would trade positions ever few hours. One day prior to the trip, the two assigned flight engineers would perform a preflight inspection of the mission designated aircraft. This preflight would include a visual walk around of the aircraft, a systems check, which required the operation of the engine cowl flaps, full travel of the electrically operated propellers, etc. The most time consuming portion of this preflight was a Military Air Transport Service (MATS) requirement that on all overwater flights the aircraft fuel tanks were required to be "dipped." This required one of the engineers to walk out onto the wings, open the fuel caps for each wing tank, and using a calibrated dip stick, actually measure and record the quantity of fuel in each tank. The readings were then compared to the fuel gage readings at the engineer station on the flight deck to ensure accuracy. Any deficiencies discovered during the preflight inspection would be reported to maintenance, so that the aircraft would be ready for the next day's flight. This inspection lasted approximately four hours.

DAY 1 - TAKE OFF AND TEN AND A HALF HOURS TO HAWAII:

On the day of the planned take off, a cursory preflight was performed by the flight engineer designated as the "scanner" for the first leg of the flight. The engineer required to perform the take-off would calculate the necessary take off and landing data. This included engine take-off power settings, take off distance, climb, cruise power, and airspeed requirements. The calculations were performed using a slide rule. This may seem like an outmoded device in this age of personal computers and hand held calculators, but at the time it was considered "high-tech". The take-off data information was culled from the aircraft performance data manual, utilizing temperature, dew point, pressure altitude, wind direction and speed, and aircraft weight. The results of these calculation were then placed on what was called a "TOLD" (Take Off and Landing Data) card. A copy of this four by six inch card was passed onto the pilot for review and use as required. The engineer would then proceed to the aircraft and assist, if required, in the preflight inspection. Both engineers would discuss the aircraft loading configuration as well as weight and balance data with the loadmaster assigned to the flight crew. As can be seen, the age of the computer has significantly reduced the workload of all crewmembers in flight planning.

A short flight to Travis Air Force Base, California was almost always required to pick up cargo. Once the cargo had been uploaded, the aircraft inspected, the cargo loading checked, and the take-off and landing data calculated, it was then time to start the long series of flights that would ultimately take us to our final destination, which was usually South Vietnam. The flights took nearly one full week to complete. By comparison, a C-17 Globemaster III could now make the same flight in less than one day.

A "blade count" was required prior to each engine start. The procedure required the flight engineer to engage the starter with the ignition off. A ground observer, in radio contact with the engineer, would count off the propeller blade rotations. If the engine was to be started within one hour of shutdown, an 8 blade count was permissible. If the engine was shut down longer than one hour a blade count of 15 was required. Once the required prop rotations had been counted off, the engineer would switch the ignition on, adjust the throttle and mixture and the huge Wasp Major engine would roar to life. The reason for the "blade count" was to ensure that a liquid lock had not developed in the lower cylinders of the engine. Oil tends to seep down into the lower cylinders of radial engines when not in use. The engine would be turned over several times (the "blade count") to ensure a liquid lock had not developed due to oil accumulation in the lower cylinders. If excessive oil had accumulated, the "blade count" would not progress passed a few rotations, as the oil within the cylinders could not be compressed by the pistons. This accumulation of oil would prevent the piston from moving further up the cylinder, thus liquid locking the engine. If a liquid lock had been detected, the oil would be drained out of the cylinders, usually by removing the lower spark plugs and allowing it to drain out of the open plug holes. If the "blade count" were not performed, and excessive oil had accumulated, the engine could sustain serious damage if an attempt were made to start it.

When the blade count was complete, the ignition was switched on, and the engineer engaged the engine primer switch until between 800 to 1000 RPM was sustained. The engine primer was then released as the engine was started and running on its own. A careful check of the engine instruments was accomplished, oil pressure OK, throttle and mixture set, all gages in the green. Eventually all four engines were running, the engine start checklist completed and reported to the pilot. Upon completion of the engine start checklist, the second engineer assigned to the flight would enter the flight deck, open the navigator hatch, and position himself so that his upper torso was exposed outside the top of the aircraft, some 25 feet above the ground. In this position the second engineer acted as a "scanner" to ensure adequate clearances exists around the aircraft for taxi and also to ensure no vehicle or personnel were approaching or may potentially approach the aircraft. With four huge 3,000 plus horsepower engines turning 17 foot diameter propellers and a wingspan of 174 feet, the potential for damage to personnel and or property was significant.

When permission was received to taxi onto the active runway for take off, the flight engineer started the before take off checklist. This extensive list of items required a complete check on the health of each engine. When complete, the engineer would close the engine cowl flaps, (the Wasp Major was an air cooled engine, the cowl flaps were used to maintain engine cylinder head temperatures by controlling the flow of air through the engine compartment), set take off power (based on previous calculations performed), and when the engine's reached the correct temperature the engineer simply state, over the intercomm, "GO."

Ensuring the engines reached the correct temperature was critical, an engine that was too cool would result in lower than predicted power output, an engine too warm at the start of the take off roll could overheat during maximum power setting, with the potential for catastrophic failure. The pilot released the brakes, and the first leg of the journey was started. The flight engineer continuously scanned his control panel, monitoring the performance of the aircraft systems. If significant problems developed during the take-off roll, the engineer would call out "Abort' over the intercomm. Depending on the distance remaining, the pilot made the decision to continue the take-off roll or abort the attempt.

During take off and climb out, the second engineer aboard, the "scanner," would be in the main cabin visually observing the engines for any sign of trouble. Throughout the climb out phase, the scanner would perform an internal walk around of the aircraft. This would include entering the lower compartments under the cabin floor to check on the condition of the Auxiliary Power Unit (APU), and also to open hatches that lead out into the wings to check for signs of trouble such as fuel leaks. These passageways would allow the engineer to actually repair an engine in flight. By climbing out into these narrow passages, an engineer would first reach the main landing gear, which would be in the up and locked position. If maintenance on the inboard engine was required, the engineer would climb forward and over the landing gear assembly to get to the engine firewall door. If access to the outboard engines were require, the engineer would crawl past the landing gear to reach the outboard engines. Once at the engine, the firewall door could be lowered to gain access to the accessories mounted on the rear of the engine. If one or both of the main landing gears could not be lowered for landing, the engineer again could climb out into the wing and, using a prying device, physically unlock the gear allowing gravity to extend it into the down and locked position. Unfortunately to unlock the right hand landing gear the engineer had to crawl pass the landing gear to get to the unlocking mechanism on the outboard side of the gear. From a safety standpoint the engineer would remain in the wing for landing, as climbing back into the aircraft over the open landing gear well was not considered very safe.

Once at altitude, the pilot would call for cruise power, and the engineer would set the engine throttles and mixtures for the best possible power settings to maintain airspeed and altitude, while at the same time ensuring the best fuel/air mixture into the engine. Settled into cruise, the aircrew faced ten to twelve hours of monotonous boredom. With the autopilot on, the pilot and co pilot were resigned to monitor the radios and flight instruments. The navigator every half hour or so would check the aircraft position. This could be accomplished on later versions of the C-124C via a LORAN set. This acronym stood for Long Range Aerial Navigation, and was used to identify the aircraft location via electronic means as opposed to relying on using a sextant to "shoot the stars" as in older aircraft types. Of course, neither method was as accurate nor an easy to use as the current GPS and INS systems. The flight engineer would continue to work throughout the flight. The engines would be monitored continually for any abnormal condition, the fuel mixtures would be adjusted each half hour to ensure maximum fuel efficiency and the aircraft's performance would be plotted on a special graph.

The flights although extremely monotonous were at times punctuated with concern and excitement. One such flight took place in the early 1970's and involved a Globemaster II enroute from Travis to Hickam Air Force Base in Hawaii. Approximately eight hours into the ten or so hour planned flight a call was received over the radio (Guard channel) that a single engine private plane was experiencing engine problems. The pilot was flying solo from California to Hawaii, the engine started to lose oil pressure, and the pilot knew he could not make landfall. All craft within the immediate area were diverted to the approximate location of the small plane. Soon afterward the pilot reported that the engine had quit. The Globemaster remained on station searching the area for three hours, finally departing due to concerns over low fuel state. Upon landing at Hickam, the plane had flown a total of 15 hours, and unfortunately the missing plane and pilot were never recovered.

From a low flying, slow moving aircraft Hawaii is absolutely beautiful. The lush greenery contrasts sharply with the blue sky and bluish green ocean to form a picture perfect view on sunny days out of the flight deck windows. The long 2,394 mile flight to Hawaii required an overnight stay for the crew to rest, and aircraft servicing prior to the next flight. Hickam Air Base is rather unique from an historical standpoint. In October of 1985, the Secretary of the Interior designated Hickam AFB as a National Historic Landmark, recognizing it as one of the nations most significant historic resources associated with World War II in the Pacific. The Pacific Air Forces Headquarters building contains bullet scarred walls that have been carefully preserved. The American flag that flew over the base on December 7, 1941 is on display in the Headquarters building. A tour of these buildings on base as well as the Arizona Memorial provides one with a reminder of the need for remaining militarily prepared and vigilant for any eventuality.

DAY 2 - DESTINATION WAKE ISLAND, 2300 MILES AND 11.5 HOURS:

At daybreak the process of getting the aircraft airborne was repeated, preflight inspection (only a visual inspection this time, the more intense inspection of the initial pre mission preflight was not required). Once at cruise altitude the crew would again settle down into individual routines. With the loadmaster once each hour checking the cargo tie down chains and straps for security. If air turbulence was encountered the tie downs would be check more often. One of the items the flight engineer would check each 15 minutes would be the electrical condition of each engine. The upper portion of the flight engineer station contained an oscilloscope that was used to check on the condition of the spark plugs, ignition leads, and magnetos. Each of the C-124's four Wasp Major engine's had 28 cylinders, 56 spark plugs, and four magnetos. Each engine could consume as much as 20 gallons of oil on a ten hour flight.

A condition called "prop overspeed" was always of utmost concern to the flight engineer. This condition occurred when a propeller would start spinning at a very high RPM. If left unchecked, the propeller or a propeller blade could and would separate from the engine. If that occurred, the potential for catastrophic aircraft failure was great. If a blade separated from the engine, it could be thrown into the cabin or into the adjacent engine. The missing blade would then create an unbalanced condition, which would cause the engine to separate from the aircraft. If the complete propeller separated from the engine it could potentially strike any portion of the aircraft or other engines. With the complete propeller missing, the engine could overspeed and destroy itself. A propeller overspeed would usually be the result of a defect in the propeller pitch control system. If the propeller attempted to enter reverse pitch while in flight, the flight engineer would become aware of this initially by a Reverse Tel-Light illumination on his main control panel. This would be followed by a yawing of the aircraft (into the problem propeller) and/or the sound of a propeller overspeeding. The emergency procedure for a prop overspeed was to immediately call "PROP OVERSPEED" over the intercomm, while at the same time shutting the engine down and feathering the propeller. The pilots' action was to pull the control stick aft, thus slowing the aircraft and changing the direction of flight. This maneuver would hopefully reduce the propellers spin rate.

The 2300 mile trip took roughly elevn and a half hours, cruising at 8,500 feet. Arrival at Wake was usually uneventful, with a long slow approach to the island's single 9,850 foot concrete runway. Not much was available for entertainment. A bowling alley, snack bar, out door movie theater, and something called a "golf course" was all the fun one could expect. Not much vegetation existed; however, the sunrises and sunsets were spectacular. One could get a great nights rest on Wake. The sound of the surf crashing ashore can place a person in a very relaxed mood.

The "U" shaped island averages approximately 12 feet above sea level, with the highest point on the island about 21 feet. Wake is less than 3 square miles of coral atoll. The island was developed by Pan American World Airways in the 1930's as a base for its famous flying boats. Pan Am built a seaplane base with a repair facility and radio station. Later the military built a runway and stationed a fighter unit and marine detachment on the island. Some significant fighting took place over control of the island during the second world war, and after the war ended, two monuments were dedicated commemorating those fallen during the battle over the island. A U.S. Marine Memorial and a Japanese Memorial both stand in close proximity to one another commemorating those on both sides who gave their lives for their countries. Commercial aircraft have not used the island since the introduction of jet transports, with their inherent long range, they now overfly the island.

DAY 3 - ONTO THE PHILLIPINE ISLANDS, ABOUT 13.5 HOURS:

The flight out of Wake required an early morning take-off. The high temperatures, and humidity, coupled with the relatively short runway (9,850 feet long by 150 feet wide) at 13 feet above sea level were always a matter of concern for heavily loaded aircraft. After the required preflight inspection and performance calculations, the take off from Wake always contained the proverbial "pucker factor." The long take off roll over a short runway caused lift off and climb out relatively low over the water for some distance. With sharks plentiful in the waters surrounding the island, everyone aboard would coach the aircraft higher until a comfortable distance and altitude were arrived at.

The flight from Wake to the Philippine Islands took about thirteen and a half hours. The crew settled into routines. Although early C-124A's carried a radio operator, with the advent of relatively modern communications gear, the C-124C version did not require the extra crewmember, and associated gear. This allowed for more space on the flight deck. Late in the aircraft's life its airspeed was restricted to under 200 KIAS, or about 230 MPH. This reduction in airspeed was required due to a structural problem associated with the outboard wing panels. Reports indicated that the wing panels could depart the aircraft at airspeeds above 230 KIAS. This slow speed, coupled with the relatively low cruise altitude, (averaging 7,000 to 13,000 feet MSL), as well as the constant vibrations of the airframe, lead to crew fatigue after several hours of flight. This was one of the reasons that the aircraft carried two flight engineers. After a four hour stint at the control panel, the engineers would change positions.

The flight engineer kept relatively busy during these long overwater flights. "Low Cruise Flight" (engines operating below 1500 Brake Horse Power) would tend to fowl the 56 spark plugs in each engine. This was due to aviation grade gasoline (115/145) containing as much as 4.6 cc of lead per gallon. Deposits would build up on the plugs that, if left unattended, would foul them, rendering the plug lifeless. This would, as can be expected, greatly reduce engine performance. To prevent this, a periodic defouling was accomplished by the engineer. The procedure required the engineer to:

> Move the mixture lever to the Rich/Normal position.
> Using performance calculations, establish the required RPM for 1800-1900 BHP.
> Move the throttle slowly (3 to 5 seconds per inch of mani fold pressure) until manifold pressure for 1800 - 1900 BHP is established.
> Hold 1800 - 1900 BHP for 5 minutes.
> Return to former cruise settings.
> For cruise above 1500 BHP, defouling was not required. The engineer would scan the engine analyzer for correct patterns once each hour. If the analyzer indicated foul plug(s), the engineer would defoul as follows:
> Mixture lever to Rich/Normal position.
> Reduce power until the spare plug(s) resume firing, and operate at that power for at least 1 minute.
> Establish RPM for 1800 - 1900 BHP (3 to 5 seconds per 100 RPM)
> Move throttle slowly (3 to 5 seconds per inch of manifold pressure) until manifold pressure for 1800 - 1900 BHP is established.
> Hold 1800 - 1900 BHP for 5 minutes.
> Return to former cruise settings.

During the defouling procedure, the engine analyzer pattern would be observed to ensure the spark plug(s) were clean. If a misfire occurred at any point in the defouling procedure, power would have to be reduced until the plug(s) resumed firing, then the procedure would continue.

The flight engineer was required to monitor the aircraft's flight performance during each leg of the mission. This was accomplished using the Aircraft Performance Log. Each half hour the engineer was required to enter a wide variety of parameters, such as air temperature, engine horsepower, fuel used, gross weight, etc. into the log. Once all the required parameters were entered, computations were accomplished to arrive at an "end gross weight". By comparing the end gross weight to the actual computed gross weight a delta gross weight, if any, would be arrived at. The completed forms were sent to the squadron chief flight engineer, who was responsible for analysis of the information. The chief flight engineer was required to contact the next higher headquarters if a deterioration in the performance of a specific aircraft was detected. The performance log was a very useful tool for the engineer. Once on a flight from Travis AFB, California to Hickam AFB, Hawaii, a Globemaster continually registered a plus delta gross weight of 7,000 pounds (heavy). This delta confounded the engineer as well as the pilots. Upon landing a walk around inspection revealed the pilot forgot to raise the landing lights, as they were off but still in the down position. During the next leg of the mission, with the lights in the up position, the aircraft's performance matched its gross weight calculations, the delta 7,000 pounds had disappeared.

Clark Air Base in the Philippines was the largest USAF base outside of the continental United States, containing some 167,000+ acres with two 13,000 foot runways. The base was about a two hour car ride from the capitol city of Manila. It was always a treat to finally view the base from the air, knowing that within a relatively short time we would be on the ground and ready to have a great meal after the Wake Island snack bar, in flight box lunch, and the long flight itself. Housing was usually at a premium on base, so transit aircrews were housed in one of several hotels in downtown Angeles

City, just outside the base. In 1991 the USAF turned Clark Air Base over to Filipino authorities as required under terms agreed to between the US and Philippine governments. Unfortunately, the eruption of Mount Pinatubo completely destroyed most of the structures on the airbase, rendering the base unusable. Extensive repairs were accomplished, and the base is now called Clark International, and is part of the Clark Special Economic Zone established by the Philippine government.

DAY 4 - FINAL DESTINATION, SOUTH VIETNAM:

The morning of the fourth day brought concern to the aircrew, as a slow moving cargo flight into South Vietnam was not the most sought after type of flying. After a thorough inspection of the aircraft, a check of the weight and balance and completion of the required performance calculations, the aircrew was briefed on the call signs for the day, issued side arms, and advised on procedures required should the aircraft go down in-country. The take off was followed by a relatively short 900 mile or so flight that was usually uneventful until the approach into either Da Nang or Cam Ran Bay. Flights into these bases at times would be met with ground fire.

Once on the ground, aircrews were not permitted to leave the vicinity of the aircraft. The reason behind this was, of course, that such a large cargo aircraft made too tempting a target. Therefore cargo would be offloaded, and new cargo onloaded as soon as possible. Usual turn around time in country was approximately two hours. During the interm new take off and landing data was calculated, the aircraft inspected, and when cargo operations were complete the aircraft immediately departed the base.

THE RETURN TRIP:

The return flight was usually a mirror image of the inbound trip, retracing the route inbound and took about as long. Several points should be made about flying in "Old Shaky." One is that the aircraft was not pressurized, which meant that any flights above 10,000 feet required the crew to don oxygen masks. The second is that the long overwater flights created extreme boredom, which tended to wear down the overall alertness of the aircrew. This, as stated, was one of the primary reasons for carrying two flight engineers. Once seated at the flight engineer station, the engineer could not stand up or leave the immediate area. The reason being self evident, should a problem develop with one of the engines, such as a propeller overspeed, the engineer would be required to take immediate action. The engineers would change positions every four hours. This would allow the engineer departing the engineers station a chance to walk around and "stretch his legs." During long overwater trips pinochle was played extensively. It was a common practice for the loadmaster, navigator, second engineer, and relief pilot, as well as any other person on board to gather in the main cabin for several hours of cards.

Air conditioning problems were nonexistent on the aircraft, simply because it did not exist. There were no provisions for keeping the crew or passengers cool. For the aircrew on the flight deck, sometimes opening the navigator's bubble, (this was hinged on one end and latched in place on the other), at low altitudes would dropped the flight deck temperature several degrees by allowing the air to circulate out the open hatch.

On flights over the Northern Atlantic, the crew carried exposure suits. These suits resembled a loose fitting divers suit. These 1940's era suits were uncomfortable to wear, however they did provided some degree of protection from the cold waters of the North Atlantic. All aircrew members were required to perform annual water landing training that included wearing exposure suits. One additional benefit of the suit was that it trapped air within it, causing the wearer to be somewhat buoyant while in the water. The drawback was that this buoyancy made swimming to and climbing into a life raft difficult.

Under the right conditions, flights over the North Atlantic created the phenomenon called Saint Elmo's Fire. On the Globemaster I and II the phenomenon developed as a strange glow around windscreen protrusion, such was the windscreen wipers. The yellowish green glow would gradually grow in size and intensity, and last for minutes at a time. However, it would vanish with considerable speed when conditions for its existence deteriorated. One other phenomenon that could be encountered in cold wet weather was rime ice build up on the propeller hubs. The build up of ice on a rotating propeller was quite an unusual sight to see. One would not normally expect to see ice build up on an object rotating at such a velocity. However, it would when conditions were right, and the sight was fantastic to observe. Propeller heaters kept the ice from building up on the props.

On trips, military transport aircraft carried what was termed "flyaway kits". These kits consisted of items that could potentially fail during long flights. A normal kit would contain a set of landing gear tires, spark plugs, ignition lead wires, magnetos, exhaust stacks (exhaust pipes), an extra propeller synchronizer, etc. Should an aircraft develop a problem whilst on a trip, and parts were not readily available to repair the aircraft at its destination or any intermediate stop, then parts from the kit would be used to repair the aircraft.

VARIENTS

YC-124B (Douglas Model 1182E)

Only one prototype was built and flown, Air Force serial number 51-72, contractor number 43406. This was a highly modified C-124A, fitted with four Pratt & Whitney YT34-P-6 turboprop engines developing 5,500 horsepower each. The aircraft was developed in partnership with the Air Force Air Research and Development Command. The intent of the project was to provide data on the operation of turboprop aircraft and systems. The first flight of the YC-124B took place February 2, 1954. The basic C-124A structure was retained, however the vertical tail surface area was increased and strengthened. The aircraft was also pressurized, which allowed for operations at 30,000 feet. It had a cruise speed of 300 mph and a top speed of 375 mph. This was substantially higher than the reciprocating engine powered C-124C.

YKC-124B

Proposed as an in-flight refueling tanker aircraft, it never progressed passed the proposal stage. This variant would have been the same basic aircraft as the turboprop powered YC-124B, but would have carried all of the necessary internal fuel tanks and external refueling mechanisms for in-flight refueling. It is assumed that the reason this never progressed passed the proposal stage was that the KC-97 (military version of the Boeing B-377 Stratocruiser) was performing admirably as an interm tanker until a jet powered refueling aircraft came into service.

C-124C TURBOPROP TESTBED

One C-124C was modified to flight test a Pratt & Whitney T-57 turboprop engine. The aircraft was flown using the aircraft equipped R-4360 radial engines. The T-57 turboprop was mounted in the forward section of the aircraft's main cargo compartment and merely operated in flight. It was never used to actually power the aircraft.

C-124X (C-132 Globemaster III)

In 1953 the USAF issued specifications and design criteria for the C-124X aircraft. This was to be a radically redesigned version of the turboprop powered C-124B. While keeping the same YT34-P-6 powerplants, the airframe would have been modified to eliminate the nose clamshell doors. The rear of the aircraft would have been redesigned to incorporate a set of large cargo doors functioning much the same as the deleted clamshell doors. The entire rear fuselage and tail were also to be redesigned. The wings and tail surfaces were proposed to be swept back. The program was dropped without a prototype being built. A version of this design later surfaced as the Douglas C-133 Cargomaster.

6. Typical Globemaster II maintenance hanger; Hamilton AFB, CA. Giant size of the aircraft is evident in this photo. (Photo from author's collection).

7. Flight line at Hamilton AFB. Only a portion of the assigned aircraft are shown in this photo. (Photo from author's collection).

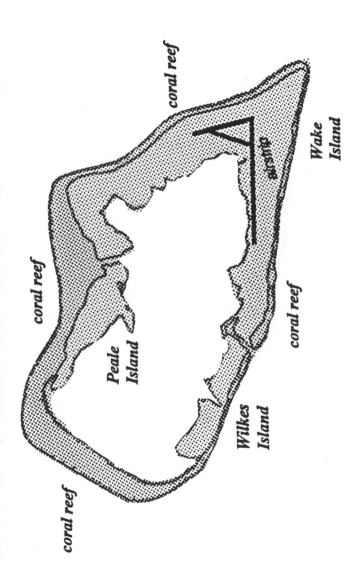

Pacific Ocean

ILLUSRTATION #1. Wake Island is actually made up of three separate islands, Wake, Peale, and Wilkes. The runway is located on Wake, which is the largest of the three islands. The total area of all three combined is approximately four square miles. There is no fresh water, and vegetation consist of shrubs and bushes.

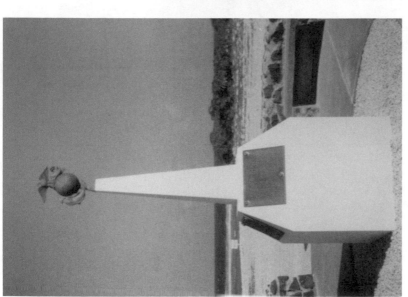

8. World War II memorials. Left photo shows the Marine Memorial, right the Japanese Memorial. Unfortunately, with the advent of modern jet transport, Wake is now overflown and consequently the Memorials are not often visited. (Photo from author's collection).

9. On the ground in Vietnam. Aircrew take a break in the bunkers located near the offloading ramp at DaNang South Vietnam. (Photo from author's collection).

10. C-124A, serial number 50-113 inflight - The weather radar had not been incorporated into the Globemaster II's during the era this photo was taken. The aircraft is unusually devoid of the glamorous paint schemes that the Military Air Transport Squadron (MATS) and the Strategic Air Command (SAC) were noted for. Snow capped Mount Fuji appears in the background. (Photo courtesy-Smithsonian)

11. Globemaster II main instrument panel layout. As with the C-74, the C-124 also lacked engine instrumentation, save for the rpm and manifold pressure instruments. All other engine instruments were at the flight engineers control panel. Note that the Douglas logo is missing from the central hub of the control wheels. These items were routinely pilfered from many Douglas transports, as they contained sentimental value to those that have flown or maintained the aircraft over the years.(Photo courtesy - Douglas)

12. View of cargo loading operations taking place in the Philippines. Photo shows the clamshell doors open, the loading ramps extended and cargo being loaded into the aircraft. During this operation an F-4 fighter horizontal stabilizer is being loaded on board. (Photo from author's collection).

13. External view of C-124C located at the Travis Air Base Museum. Large size of the aircraft can be extrapolated by comparing the aircraft to others shown. (Photo from author's collection).

14. Front quarter view of same aircraft at Travis Museum. (Photo from author's collection).

15. Interior view of a Globemaster II's main cabin. Last section of upper deck flooring has been lowered, one set of seats have been installed. The reciprocating engine Globemasters could carry 200 fully equipped combat troops. Overhead traveling crane can be seen in the upper right hand portion on photo. Also visible are the loading ramps in the up and stowed position. (Photo from author's collection).

16. Loading platform in operation. After a long mission to Southeast Asia, aircrew were glad to get their belongings and be off to their families.

17. Extremely large cargo could be carried in the Globemaster II. Photo shows a US Army communications trailer being loaded for a trip to West Germany. (Photo from author's collection).

Chapter III
TRILOGY COMPLETE,
THE GLOBEMASTER III

The C-17A Globemaster III completes the Globemaster trilogy. This aircraft could conceivably become the consummate airlifter. The aircraft was designed by Douglas as a strategic airlifter capable of carrying heavy outsized cargo into austere airfields anywhere in the world. In keeping with modern aircraft of this era, it can be refueled in flight, extending its range significantly. The wing incorporates the "supercritical airfoil" design, this coupled with winglets at each wingtip significantly increase fuel efficiency. With its 3 man crew, the aircraft can fly 3,000 miles without refueling at 0.77 Mach while carrying 102 troops or 172,000 pounds of cargo. Normal cruise speed is Mach 0.74 at 28,000 feet. It has a service ceiling of 45,000 feet, and a ferry range of 4,700 miles.

In October of 1980, the USAF issued a "Request For Proposal" (RFP) for a new large transport aircraft. At the time of the RFP this aircraft was known as the "CX" , which stood for Cargo Experimental. The original concept was for an aircraft to replace the C-141. However, unlike the C-141, the CX would be developed for rough field operations. One of the requirements of the CX was for the aircraft to fly from any base in the U.S. non-stop to a forward located airfield anywhere in the world, using in-flight refueling. This would be quite different than the then typical heavy airlift operation which tasked a C-5 to fly from the U.S. to an air base nearest the theater of operations that could accommodate it. The cargo was then transferred to a C-130 for forward deployment.

The RFP evaluation was conducted from January through August 1981. The USAF selected McDonnell Douglas Aerospace (MDA), to develop the "next generation" cargo aircraft on the 28th of August 1981. Full Scale Development started at the Douglas Aircraft Division on 26 July 1986. Fabrication of the first aircraft started on 2 November 1987, and the production contract was issued on 20 January 1988. Assembly actually started on the prototype, serial number 87-0025, at the Douglas facility in Long Beach, California on 24 August 1988. The prototype was completed on 21 December 1990.

The aircraft was originally designed to take-off with a maximum payload of 172,000 pounds utilizing 7,600 feet of runway, fly non-stop 2,400 nautical miles and land at its destination using 3,000 feet of runway. A propulsive lift system allows the aircraft to achieve full stop landings within 3,000 feet. The system uses engine exhaust to generate lift. The exhaust is directed onto the large trailing edge flaps which extend into the exhaust stream allowing the aircraft to fly a steep approach at a relatively low landing speed. Fully loaded, the aircraft was originally designed to back up a 2.5% slope using engine thrust reversers. The production C-17A has an empty weight of 277,000 pounds, and a gross weight of 580,000 pounds. One other design feature of the aircraft is that it is capable of turning in a very small radius, and can complete a 180 degree turn in just 80 feet. This small turn radius allows the aircraft to fly into small austere airfields.

Unlike previous Globemaster's, the C-17 is produced as a partnership with other aircraft manufacturers. The major subcontractor on the program is Northrop Grumman, responsible for the manufacture of the engine nacelles, vertical and horizontal stabilizer, ailerons, elevators, and rudders. The Globemaster III incorporates approximately 16,000 pounds of composite structures, panels and skins, which make the aircraft stronger, lighter, and more reliable than an all metallic aircraft. Major portions of the fuselage and wing are graphite epoxy. The engine nacelles are made of aluminum, titanium, high-strength steel and graphite epoxy/polyimide composites. The ailerons, elevators, and rudders are graphite epoxy.

Controversy surrounded the Globemaster III during test and evaluation. Problems with meeting the original contract requirements generated proposals from Boeing Aircraft for a military version of the 747 Freighter. Although on the surface this proposal appeared to be attractive, the aircraft would have had to have been extensively modified to carry the heavy loads such as tanks and other tracked vehicles that the C-17 was designed for. Additionally the austere airfield's requirement would not have been met with the Boeing 747 as designed. In an unusual twist of fate, Boeing and McDonnell Douglas merged in 1997. Boeing then pursued the commercialization of the C-17, seeking to have the FAA certify the MD-17, (the civilian version of the C-17), as a heavy outsized commercial freight hauler. In another unusual twist to the Globemaster story, the Globemaster I was originally designed as a civilian passenger aircraft, and when the civilian version did not materialize, the US Military requested it be converted into a troop and cargo transport. The Globemaster II was never considered for anything other than a military cargo transport. We now end the Globemaster trilogy with the reverse, the Globemaster III starting life as a military transport, and being converted for civilian use. There will be some changes to the civilian version, for example, the air-to-air refueling capability, military avionics, and air drop capabilities of the C-17 will be dropped. The MD-17 will incorporate a commercial cargo floor, which will aid in the rapid installation commercial cargo containers.

Due to problems associated with production and program management, the program was transferred in 1992 from Douglas Long Beach to MDA's Military Aircraft Division in St. Louis. The aircraft production line remained in Long Beach, with overall program responsibility residing with management in St. Louis. The initial requirement of 210 aircraft was cut to 120 in 1991. In January 1994 the program requirement was capped at 40 aircraft for 2 years. This cut was deemed necessary by DOD to ensure contractor requirements to achieve performance, cost, and delivery targets were met.

The green light for more aircraft was subsequently given by the Department of Defense for 120 aircraft, to be delivered through the year 2004. This contract increase to 120 aircraft was partially vindicated by the 1997 Quadrennial Defense Review (QDR) Report which stated that to meet military obligations, no fewer than 120 C-17's would be required. The airlift plan calls for the replacement of the 256 aircraft C-141 Starlifter fleet with a 120 aircraft C-17 fleet. The last C-141 aircraft will be retired from the Active Forces in 2003, and plans call for the last Reserve aircraft will be retired in 2006. These figures did not include 13 special operations C-141's that will remain operational until a successor is designated. The C-17 again seems the logical choice, as it is equipped with a night vision goggles capable flight deck, and is larger than the Starlifter. If it is picked to replace the special operations C-141, then an additional quantity buy will be required in addition to the current 120 aircraft.

The first flight test aircraft flew from the Douglas facility in Long Beach to the Flight Test Center at Edwards Air Force Base in California (approximately 100 miles from Long Beach) on September 15, 1991. The flight lasted 2.5 hours, with the aircraft flying at 20,000 feet, 250 knots and carrying 20,000 pounds of concrete blocks to maintain the proper center of gravity. Numerous equipment checks were conducted during the flight. From September 1991 through December 1994 the C-17 completed 5,623 flight test data points and 1,028 ground test points during its testing phase at Edwards AFB. Approximately 4,400 flight hours were amassed, with the aircraft logging over 1300 flights. An additional 1350 hours of ground testing was also accomplished during the testing period. Additional operational testing was then accomplished at Fort Hood, Texas and Pope AFB, North Carolina. This testing phase consisted of airdrops, air refueling, loading and unloading as well as cargo and passenger flights. The testing at Pope consisted of aircraft strategic airlift, static ground testing, austere airfield operations, low velocity airdrops, paratroops airdrops, container system deliveries, and unpaved airfield operation. During testing the aircraft performed landings on the dry lake bed at Edwards AFB. Rough field landings were accomplished on an aluminum matted Marine Corps expeditionary airfield at Twenty Nine Palms in the California desert. The aircraft also landed on a dirt strip at Bicycle Lake, California. During the testing phase the C-17 set 22 world records, including payload to altitude time-to-climb, and a short takeoff and landing record in which it took off in less than 1,400 feet carrying a payload of 44,000 pounds. The C-17 flew 165 sorties totaling close to 400 flight hours. The testing concluded that the aircraft was capable of meeting the needs of the military services.

The first production C-17A was delivered in June of 1993 to the 17th Airlift Squadron of the 437th Airlift Wing at Charleston AFB, South Carolina, and was promptly named the *"Spirit of Charleston."* The aircraft was delivered one year late to the contract and arrived with 100 contract waivers and deviations. To celebrate the U.S. Air Forces 50th anniversary, the 34th aircraft delivered to the 437th Airlift Wing, during the first week of October 1997 was designated *"The Spirit of the Air Force".*

The 35th C-17A was delivered to the 437th Wing on November 14,1997. The 97th Air Mobility Wing at Altus Air Force Base, Oklahoma received its 8th and final aircraft on November 10th, 1997. This was the first unit to acquire its full complement of aircraft. A significant flight hour mark was passed when the total C-17 fleet passed the 70,000 flight hour mark in November of 1997.

A tribute of sort was paid to the C-17A when US President Clinton flew on a C-17 into Bosnia to visit the US contingent to the United Nations peace keeping and stabilization force in Bosnia. The flight capped an eventful 1997 for the Globemaster in that during the year a C-17A was dedicated to Bob Hope, the longest airdrop mission in history occurred of which the C-17 took part, and the 24th consecutive aircraft was delivered ahead of schedule to the Air Mobility Command.

C-17's are equipped with in-flight refueling capability. This allows the aircraft to operate from the continental U.S. without stopping at an intermediate staging base. The aircraft is also equipped with Global Positioning System (GPS) technology. The GPS coupled with information from the U.S. Space Command satellite imagery information provides aircrews with the ability to chart, with extreme accuracy, the timing of airdrops. This navigational accuracy allows airdrops to an area measured in feet. Prior to GPS, airdrops were judged accurate if the cargo fell within tens of yards of the drop zone. The aerial delivery of supplies has allowed mission commanders considerable leeway in maintaining logistics support of troops on the ground. The aircraft can airdrop a total of eleven model 463L pallets, 110,000 pounds can be sequentially airdropped, or a single load of 60,000 pounds.

Automatic cargo locks built into the main cabin flooring aid in releasing cargo during airdrops, making the operation much safer and faster than previous methods. Command and Control has also gone high tech with the installation of a SATCOM radio link. This capability allows the aircrew and/or passengers the capability to communicate with anyone anywhere on the planet at any time.

In May of 1995, the National Aeronautic Association honored the U.S. Air Force, McDonnell Douglas (now a division of The Boeing Company), the U.S. Army, and the C-17 Industrial Team with the prestigious Collier Trophy for the year 1994. The Trophy was awarded for design, development, testing, producing, and placing into service the Globemaster III. The Collier Trophy was established in 1911, and is awarded each year by the National Aeronautic Association for the greatest achievements in aeronautics or astronautics in America, the value of which has been demonstrated the previous year.

Following in the Globemaster tradition, the aircraft was designed for conversion from cargo to aeromedical or maximum passenger loading's. In the aeromedical roll, it has the capability of carrying a total of 102 ambulatory patients non-stop from anywhere in the world to any hospital in the U.S. In the troop transport roll, it can be converted to carry a maximum of 154 passengers. In actuality, these figures closely resemble the airlift capabilities of the Globemaster II. The C-124C was capable of carrying a maximum of 200 combat troops. It could also be configured to carry a maximum of 127 litter patients. Of course one of the major differences being in the speed (transit time) to destination.

During an exercise code named *Centrazbat 97,* C-17A's flew non-stop from Fort Bragg, North Carolina to the Kazakhstan Republic, a distance of approximately 8,000 miles. The September 14th through 15th 1997 mission took nearly 20 hours and required 3 in-flight refuelings. The C-17A's were part of an 8 aircraft flight that carried a total of 500 paratroops from the 82nd Airborne Division and 40 Central Asian troops. Two of the Globemaster III's airdropped vehicles and cargo. It took a mere seven seconds to airdrop two Humvee vehicles out of the rear cargo door of one C-17A. The drop was accomplished at approximately 140 MPH. This was the first time the C-17A had performed such a mission. The joint exercise was designed for training in the deployment of peacekeepers, and was conducted with 1,400 troops from the U.S., Russia, Turkey, Georgia, Kazakhstan, Kyrgyzstan, Uzbekistan, and Latvia. The exercise lasted 6 days and included MIG-29 fighters from the Kazakhstani Republic.

Summary of Selected Aircraft Systems:

Flight Controls

The C-17 is the first military transport to incorporate a fully digital "fly-by-wire" flight control system. Starting with the F-16 and F/A-18 in the late 1970's, new aircraft were designed with electronically operated flight control systems. On the Globemaster I and II, (and other pre-1970's production aircraft), the flight control systems were operated by mechanical linkages attached directly from the pilots control stick to the flight control surfaces, or to hydraulic actuators. As the pilot moved the control stick, a set of cables, pulleys, bellcranks, etc. moved from the cockpit to the control surfaces. As can be expected, this required considerable effort on the pilots part for an aircraft the size of the C-124, although an independent aileron boost system was available and could be selected by the pilot. In the "fly-by-wire" system, the direct mechanical link between the control stick in the cockpit and the control surfaces has been eliminated for normal operations. In the C-17, the pilot moves the control stick and/or rudder pedals to change the direction of flight. This movement is converted into an electronic signal which is routed to a Quadruple Redundant Lockheed Martin Digital Computer System. The computers take into account a set of parameters such as airspeed, altitude, gross weight, etc., and then routes an electronic signal to the respective flight control hydraulic servocylinders, which then act to reposition the corresponding control surface accordingly.

The C-17's flight control system also contains an emergency mechanical back-up system. This system is inactive until selected by the pilot. If engaged, it allows the pilot to fly the aircraft via a direct link from the control stick to the flight control hydraulic servocylinders. The system is only intended to be used if there is a problem with the electronic flight control system, or if a complete electrical system failure has been experienced. Test pilots who have flown the aircraft with the emergency mechanical back up system engaged say that the aircraft handles well, except for being slightly sluggish when compared to flights with the electronic system. One other difference between older transport aircraft and the C-17 is the pilots control stick. On older aircraft the control stick was a control column with a yoke, or steering wheel, attached. On the C-17 the control column now resembles that of a fighter aircraft, in that it has a control stick or joy stick, the yoke has been eliminated. Pilots report that this actually make the C-17 easier, and more user friendly to fly as compared to the older styled aircraft.

Actual flight control surfaces consist of:
One set of ailerons installed on the outboard wing panels
Four spoilers per wing
Four elevator sections
Two surface rudders, sectioned as upper and lower rudders
Full span leading edge slats
Two-slot fixed vane hinged trailing edge flaps
Empennage strakes

The wing flaps are considered part of the "powered lift' system. This system enables the aircraft to perform slow, steep landing approaches with heavy cargo loads. The steep approach allows the pilot to make precision landings on short runways. This is accomplished by utilizing the trailing edge wing flaps to divert engine exhaust downward, giving the wing increased lift. The system generates about twice the lift coefficient of conventional wing flap systems.

Cargo Handling

The cargo compartment has been designed to allow the C-17 to carry a wide range of vehicles. It has a sufficiently large cross section to transport wheeled and tracked vehicles such as tanks, trucks, helicopters, and artillery as well as the Patriot missile system. The aircraft can carry the Sheridan tank or the Bradley fighting vehicle. It can carry three Bradley's in one load, as well as airdrop them. The airlift capabilities of the aircraft include a combat offload of up to 18 pallets (69,000 pounds), a Container Delivery System capable of airdropping up to 40 containers, weighing 2,350 pounds each. It is also capable of offloading up to 102 paratroopers. One special feature incorporated into the offload system is the LAPES system. This acronym stands for Low Altitude Parachute Extraction System, which allows cargo to be offloaded while the aircraft is flown only a few feet above the ground.

All major cargo handling is accomplished via the rear cargo loading doors. There are two clamshell doors and a loading ramp mounted on the rear of the aircraft. The doors and ramp are electronically actuated and hydraulically operated. The aircraft loadmaster is provided with a control station in the forward section of the main cabin. From this station the loadmaster can perform the necessary weight and balance calculations, and oversee cargo loading as required. Additionally, the station allows the loadmaster the capability to monitor the load in flight. The main cabin floor incorporates the standard tie-down rings, as well as a new electronically operated metallic tie-down strip. This strip allows for a standard C-17 cargo container to be retained in the aircraft without the usual tie-down straps and or chains. A cargo container is loaded onto the aircraft and, when properly positioned, the loadmaster throws a switch which actuates the retaining strip. The strip rises from the main cabin floor and latches onto a set of metal protrusions on the base of the container, thereby holding it securely in place.

Cockpit Instrumentation

The C-17 was designed from the outset as a "glass cockpit" aircraft. The term "glass cockpit" refers to the elimination of the standard instrumentation, commonly referred to as "steam gage" instruments, in favor of multi-functioned electronic. The flight deck main instrument panel consists of four multi-function electronic displays, and two full time all functioning heads up displays. This in addition to some conventional "steam gage" back-up instrumentation.

The navigation system is composed of digital electronics, and the communications system has been designed as an integrated radio management system. The glass cockpit, coupled with the outstanding integration of systems on the aircraft are the major reasons why this aircraft only requires a pilot and co-pilot on the flight deck.

Defensive Systems

The aircraft carries the ALE-47 chaff flare countermeasure dispensers as well as the AAR-47 missile warning system. The AAR-47 system detects heat emitted by the exhaust of missiles during the launch and boost phase. The system is composed of a set of thermal sensors with four photomultipliers, a signal processing unit, and a cockpit mounted control indicator. The photomultipliers provide the aircraft with full 360 degree coverage. The system provides the aircrew with a warning, via the cockpit indicator, of a missile launch as well as the missile direction from the aircraft. Once detected, a signal is automatically sent to the ALE-47 countermeasures dispenser, which then dispenses expendable countermeasures to lure the missile away from the aircraft. The mode of operation can be fully automatic, semi-automatic, or manual. A cockpit control set allows the aircrew to select the mode of operation required for the threat environment. The system can dispense flares to lure heat seeking missiles away from the aircraft engine exhaust. It can also dispense chaff (metallic strips of varying length), which foils electronic sensors such as radar, thus greatly reducing the chance that the aircraft will be hit by a radar guided missile.

Fuel System:

As in previous Globemaster's, the C-17 fuel storage system is contained within the wings. The storage system consists of two outboard wing tanks for a total of 5,603 gallons per wing or 11,206 total., and two inboard wing tanks for a total of 7,940 gallons per wing or 15,880 total. Total fuel capacity is 27,086 gallons, or 181,476 pounds. Fuel transfer is accomplished automatically via a mission computer operating electric fuel transfer and feed pumps. Manual control of the fuel transfer system is also available to the pilots should a fuel imbalance develop during flight. If an electrical problem develops rendering the electric fuel transfer and feed system inoperative, the fuel valves are designed to fail to the open position allowing fuel to gravity flow to the engines.

C-17 CIVILIAN AIRLIFT OPERATIONS

Although the Globemaster III is the newest USAF airlifter, it has performed quite a few humanitarian airlift operations since entering operational use. The following summarize some of the accomplishments this aircraft has performed in assisting the world in maintaining peace and removing personnel from harms way:

1995 - In September hurricane Marilyn, with winds up to 110 mph, devastated sections of Puerto Rico and also St. Thomas in the Virgin Islands. C-17's, carrying relief supplies flew to the areas of devastation. Also carried were a large quantity of outsized items that the U.S. Army needed to help rebuild the infrastructure of the islands.

1995 - In December Globemasters , supporting Operation Provide Promise, flew relief missions into Bosnia to assist that civil war torn country's populace recover from the horrors of war. In one day, December 8th, at the Sarajevo airport, one C-17 offloaded 154,000 pounds of gas heaters and pressed wood in less than 35 minutes.

1996 - On February 2nd, a C-17 departed Travis AFB, CA on a 14.5 hour non-stop flight to Tuzla Air Base, Bosnia. The aircraft carried 40 tons of fence posts needed to mark mine fields within that country, thus aiding in reducing death and dismemberment civilians were sustaining by wandering into unmarked mine fields.

1996 - In April of this year a Globemaster was dispatched to Dubrovnik, Croatia to pick up the remains of Commerce Secretary Ron Brown and other members of the Commerce mission to Bosnia and Herzegovina.

1996 - Aircrews from the 437th and 315th Airlift Wings at Charleston AFB, SC provided airlift support to war refugees fleeing into neighboring Zaire. Continued support of the Zaire relief effort saved uncounted civilian lives.

1998 - C-17 crews delivered electrical repair personnel and equipment to Maine after severe winter storms disrupted life in the state.

18. C-17 in flight. A true work of art. (Photo courtesy Boeing)

19. Front view of the C-17. (Photo courtesy Boeing)

20. Main instrument panel of the C-17. Note fighter type control stick, computer screens and heads up display. The high tech Globemaster has arrived. (Photo from author's collection).

21. Interior view of the C-17 main cabin. View shows the wing carry through box, which reduces the internal height in this area by 20 inches. Photo is view looking aft from mid point of the flight deck ladder. (Photo from author's collection).

Chapter IV
POWERPLANTS
THE GLOBEMASTER I & II

The engines that powered the Globemaster I and II were the largest aircraft production reciprocating engines manufactured in the U.S. The R-4360 engines on these aircraft produced anywhere from 3,000 to 3,800 horsepower each, depending on the version. The R-4360 was manufactured by Pratt & Whitney Aircraft Engines and was officially called the Wasp Major. However, unofficially it was called the "Corn Cob," a term coined due to the multiple rows of 28 cylinders arranged in 4 rows of 7 cylinders each, thus from the side it had the appearance of a very large corn cob. The engine was an air cooled 4 cycle radial with a cylinder bore of 5.8 inches and a stroke of 6 inches. There were 2 spark plugs per cylinder for a total of 56 spark plugs per engine. During operation, 14 cylinders would fire with each engine revolution. Maximum horsepower was produced at about 2,700 RPM. Each engine had an oil tank that held a total of 82.5 gallons. During an average 10 hour flight, it was not unusual for an engine to consume 20 gallons of oil. The Wasp Major had its origins in 1925 when Pratt & Whitney designed and fabricated, within 7 months, the R-1340 Wasp, an engine producing 400 horsepower. The original Wasp R-1340 was followed by ever increasingly larger and more powerful radial engines culminating in the R-4360 Wasp Major.

The engines that powered the final version of the C-124C Globemaster II, was the R 4360-63A (Pratt & Whitney model B-6). Each engine incorporated a two speed supercharger, a

Bendix Stromberg pressure injection carburetor, and an Antidetenation (ADI) system. Each of the 4 engines was equipped with 4 low tension magneto's. Each magneto provided current to a set of spark plugs in each of two rows of cylinders. The superchargers were controlled by switches mounted on the flight engineers station. Selection of High Blower energized a 28 volt dc solenoid which directed engine oil to the supercharger's high blower coupling, allowing for more power to be produced at a given altitude. Selection of the low blower position de-energized the solenoid and allowed spring tension to return the supercharger coupling to the low blower position.

Engine Sections - For descriptive purposes, the engine was divided up into three major sections, consisting of:

    Front Section - Comprising the Propeller Shaft Case Section

    Power Section - Comprising the Magneto Drive Case Section, Crankcase Section, and Cylinders

    Rear Section - Consisting of the Collector Case Section, and the Accessory Drive Case Section

Engine Subsystems:

    ADI System (water/alcohol injection) - ADI permitted a safe increase in maximum power for takeoff. Water/alcohol injection was used on a wide variety of aircraft engines to suppress detonation, which allowed for high power operation with less fear of engine damage. The water/alcohol mixture also contained an oil emulsive corrosion preventative additive. In the Globemaster II, the ADI mixture was carried in two 30 gallon tanks. This 60 gallons was adequate for approximately 5 minutes of operation when maximum power was applied to all 4 engines. An ADI on - off switch mounted on the flight engineers console controlled the system. Four ADI pressure indicators were mounted on the flight engineers panel, and provided an indication of water pressure for each engine in pounds per square inch. A set of 2 ADI quantity indicators were also mounted on the flight engineers panel, and indicated the quantity of fluid in gallons available.

Torquemeter - Engine torque was monitored by a Torquemeter, installed on the flight engineers control panel. The Torquemeter measured engine torque delivered to the propeller shaft. This torque reading combined with the engine RPM allowed the engineer to calculate the brake horsepower output of the engine that was delivered to the propeller.

Engine Analyzer - An engine analyzer was mounted on the flight engineers overhead panel. This analyzer permitted continuous visual observation and analysis of the complete engine electrical system. This was in actuality an oscilloscope, and with the visual presentation, the flight engineer could determine the health of the engine electrical system from the magneto to the spark plugs. These observations included: A cylinder with no combustion taking place, an open primary magneto coil, magneto points out of synchronization, point bounce, etc. The analyzer could be operated on the ground or in flight.

Engine Ignition System - The ignition system of the R-4360-63A consisted of four magnetos per engine and two vibrator coils. Each magneto furnished current to a set of spark plugs in each of two rows of cylinders. The magneto consisted of an integral distributor and a low tension wiring harness with transformer coils. In operation, low voltage from the magneto was carried through the wiring harness to the transformer coils located near each set of spark plugs. The transformer coils then changed the current into high voltage. Earlier versions of the R-4360 were equipped with a seven magneto high voltage system. This system carried high voltage from the magneto directly to the spark plugs over the wiring harness, and proved to have a lower reliability than the low tension ignition system.

The flight engineer's overhead electrical panel was also equipped with four ignition selector switches. These switches allowed the engineer to test the magnetos for proper operation. They were marked On and Off with four push pull switches marked L1, L2, R1 and R2. By selecting the respective L (left) or R (right) push pull switch to the test position, labeled "Out" the respective magneto would be grounded out and the indication picked up via engine instruments and analyzer.

Engine Oil System - Each engine was equipped with an independent oil system. Oil was supplied to the engine via an 82.5 gallon oil tank remotely located on the aft side of the engine firewall. Four oil quantity indicators were available at the flight engineers control panel. Oil pressure was maintained by an engine driven oil pump mounted on the lower left side of the engine accessory section. Oil returned from the engine through a free flow oil cooler.

The flight engineer controlled oil temperature by the operation of electrically controlled engine oil cooler doors. This allowed the engineer to maintain the correct oil temperature allowing the engine to perform at optimum efficiency. The engineers station was equipped with an oil temperature gage and oil cooler door switches for each engine. The each engine oil system also contained an oil dilution system which allowed fuel under pressure from the carburetor to flow into the oil supply line, diluting the oil for cold weather starting. The diluted oil was circulated through the engine and returned to the oil tank. The fuel would eventually evaporate out of the oil after the system reached operating temperature. Oil dilution was controlled by the flight engineer through a set of four oil dilution switches. On serial number 49-243 through 51-5197 these switches were located on the flight engineers lower electrical control panel. On serial numbers 51-5198 and subsequent, they were moved to the overhead panel.

Cowl Flap System - Although not an engine system, the cowl flaps were integral to the proper operation of the engine, in that they controlled the cylinder head temperature of each engine. Since the engine was air cooled, the temperature could be controlled by allowing more or less air to flow out of the engine bay compartment through the open cowl flaps. Each engine was equipped with an electrically operated cowl flap system consisting of four full flaps and one upper half flap on each side of the engine nacelle. The cowl flaps traveled from a range of minus 4 degrees (closed) to plus 26 degrees (full open). The cowl flaps were operated by electrical switches mounted on the flight engineers lower electrical control panel. The switches were labeled Open, Off, and Closed, and were spring loaded to the Off position. Placing the switch to the desired position allowed 28 volt DC current to flow to the cowl flap motor. Momentary movement of the switches permitted for a relatively slow movement of the cowl flaps to the desired position. Approximately 30 seconds were required for the cowl flaps to travel full open to full closed, or visa versa.

Cowl flaps induced some significant drag during flight. During 4 engine cruise at 200 knots, if the cowl flaps were opened from a 5 degree setting to 6 degrees, the additional power required to overcome the additional drag would be 38.7 brake horsepower per engine.

During its service history, the R-4360 powered the following military aircraft:

Convair's B-36 Peacemaker Bomber - Powered by six R-4360-53 pusher type engines each producing 3,800 horsepower.

Convair's XC-99, a transport derivative of the B-36 Bomber - Powered by six R-4360-63A engines each producing 3,800 horsepower. Only one aircraft built and flown.

Boeing's B-50(KB) Superfortress Bomber - Powered by four R-4360-35 engines each producing 3,500 horsepower.

Northrop's XB-35 Flying Wing Bomber - Powered by four R-4360-17 and 2 R-4360-21 engines each producing approximately 3,000 horsepower.

Douglas C-74 Globemaster I Transport - Powered by four R-4360-49 engines each producing 3,250 horsepower each.

Douglas C-124 Globemaster II Transport - Powered by four R-4360-63A engines each producing 3,800 horsepower.

Fairchild's C-119C Boxcar Transport - Powered by two R-4360-20W engines each producing 3,250 horsepower.

Boeing's C-97G (KC) Stratocruiser (Tanker) - Powered by four R-4360-59 engines each producing 3,500 horsepower.

Hughes HK-1 Hercules (Spruce Goose) - Powered by eight R-4360-4 engines each producing 3,000 horsepower. Only one built and flown

Martin's AM-1 Mauler - Powered by one R-4360-4 engine producing 3,000 horsepower. Only one built and flown

Chance-Vought Corsair - The F2G-2 was powered by one R-4360-4 engine producing 3,000 horsepower. Modified F-4U, ten built with R-4360-4 engines.

Hughes FX-11 -(Un-named) - Powered by two R-4360-4 engine producing 3,000 horsepower. Only one built and flown.

Lockheed's Constitution - Powered by four R-4360-20 engines producing 3,500 horsepower each.

Pratt & Whitney R-4360-63A (Model B-6) Specifications:

Designation:	Wasp Major
Displacement:	4,360 Cubic Inches
Cylinders:	28
Cylinder Bore:	5.8 Inches
Stroke:	6 Inches
Compression Ratio:	6.7:1
Brake Horsepower:	3,800 (@ 2,700 RPM
Spark Plugs:	56 (2 Per Cylinder)
Ignition System:	4 Magneto, Low Tension
Weight (Dry):	3,682 Pounds
Diameter:	55 Inches

ENGINE R-4360
INTERNAL VIEW KEY COMPONENTS

1. Oil Transfer Bearing Ring Carrier
2. Oil Transfer Bearing
3. Oil Transfer Bearing Rings
4. Governor Drive Shaft Gear
5. Reduction Drivegear Outer Coupling
6. Spark Advance Control Valve
7. Crankcase Pressure Oil Line
8. Crankcase Front Counterweight
9. D Row Master Rod Assembly
10. Cam Small Drive Shaft Gear
11. Cam Large Drive Shaft Gear
12. Crankshaft Center Main Bearing
13. Crankshaft Oil Slinger
14. B Row Link Rod
15. Inlet Valve Pushrod
16. Inlet Valve Rocker
17. Crankshaft
18. Inlet Valve Springs
19. Inlet Valve
20. Piston Pin
21. Piston and Rings
22. Push Rod Cover
23. Impeller Drive Damper
24. Impeller Intermediate Drive
25. Impeller and Shaft Assembly
26. Accessory Drive Shaft
27. Impeller Shaft Rear Rings Breather
28. Fuel Feed Valve
29. Tachometer Drive Shaft Gear
30. Fuel Pump Drive Shaft Gear
31. Fuel Pump Intermediate Drive
32. Rear Oil Distributor Ring

33. Starter Drive Shaft Gear
34. Generator/Accessory Drive Gear
35. Rear Accessory Drive Gear
36. Oil Pressure Reducing Valve
37. Pressure Oil Strainer
38. Collector Case Oil Pump
39. Crankcase Scavenge Oil Line
40. Crankcase Scavenge Oil Pump
41. Exhaust Valve Rocker
42. Exhaust Valve Springs
43. Exhaust Valve
44. C-Row Master Rod
45. Cam Drive Gear
46. Cam
47. Exhaust Port Flanged Coupling
48. Magneto Intermediate Drive Gear
49. Propeller Shaft Reduction Drive Gear
50. Front Accessory Drive Gear
51. Torquemeter Pump
52. Front Power Section Scavenge Pump
53. Rocker Drain Scavenge Pump
54. Front Section Scavenge Pump
55. Propeller Shaft Ball Bearing
56. Propeller Shaft Roller Bearing
57. Thrust Cover
58. Propeller Shaft Thrust Nut
59. Propeller Oil Feed Tube
60. Propeller Shaft Reduction Drive Gear
61. Torquemeter Oil Pressure Transmitter
62. Magneto Drive Shaft
63. Spark Advance Oil Feed Tube
64. Magneto Drive Fixed Gear
65. Spark Advance Cylinder
66. Propeller Shaft
67. Magneto Drive Shaftgear

68. Torquemeter Master Piston
69. Oil Pressure Relief Valve
70. Propeller Shaft Reduction Support
71. Propeller Reduction Pinion Gear

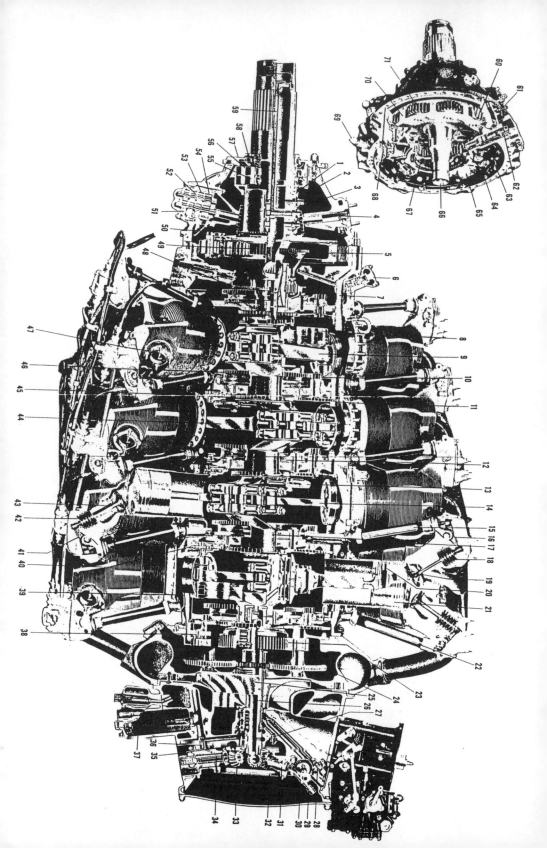

Propellers:

TYPE - The (X)C-74 utilized Curtis Electric four blade full feathering, reversible pitch constant speed propellers. Early C-124's also used the Curtis Electric propellers. However in February of 1949 an order was placed with Hamilton Standard for new propellers, and all C-124's were later fitted with the Hamilton Standard Model 23260 three bladed, 17 foot diameter, full feathering and reversible pitch constant speed props. Although the propellers were generally considered to be 17 feet in diameter, in actuality they were cut down to 16 feet 6 inches. The propeller blade was of the 2J17B3-8W design. Constant engine RPM could be maintained either manually or automatically through a 5U18 governor mounted electric propeller synchronization system.

REVERSE PITCH - The reversible pitch feature allowed the pilot to use engine power through the propellers to act as a brake. By changing the propeller pitch to the reverse position, the pilot could slow the aircraft down after landing, much like the thrust reversers on modern jet aircraft. A safety solenoid, operated by a switch on each main landing gear, prevented operation of reverse pitch while the aircraft was airborne. This meant that at least one main landing gear had to be on the ground before the safety system would allow the pilot to operate the reverse mode. Reverse pitch was one of the few engine operations that was not controlled or available to the flight engineer at his station. Reverse pitch could also be used for aircraft backing. The procedure was restricted to infrequent occasions as dictated by operational necessity. Prior to backing up, the maneuvering area was required to be free of debris that could damage the propellers or injure ground personnel. The propellers could not be held in reverse pitch longer than 1 minute. Brakes were not recommended for stopping in reverse pitch, as the aircraft could be set on its tail if excessive braking force was applied.

FEATHERING - The feathering feature allowed the flight engineer to streamline the propellers once the engine had been shut down in flight. Streamlining the propellers reduced the drag past the propeller blades. Feathering also prevented the propeller from rotating in flight due to airloads acting upon it, which in turn would create considerable drag on the aircraft. The flight engineer could feather any propeller by pulling the respective propeller selector control lever to the feather position. The propellers could also be feathered by holding the propeller selector lever in the decrease rpm position.

DEICING - Ice was prevented from building up on the propeller blades by an electrical deicing system that used heating elements externally mounted on the leading edge of each prop blade. A timer automatically controlled the length and frequency of application to the blade heaters in cycles. A complete cycle started with engine number 1 and rotated through engines 2, 3, and 4 consecutively for 15 seconds for each prop. After this cycle, no power would be applied for 60 seconds before the cycle started again. The system was controlled by 4 individual on/off switches on the flight engineers heater control panel.

22. Engine shutdown in-flight was a common occurrence during the reciprocating engine Globemaster era. (Photo from author's collection)

THE C-17A GLOBEMASTER III

The C-17A Globemaster III is powered by four Pratt & Whitney F117-PW-100 Turbofan engines. Pratt & Whitney, a division of United Technologies, was tasked with the designing and manufacturing the PW2000 series/F-117 series engine. The F-117 engine is an outgrowth of a program called the Commercial Derivative Engine (CDE). The intent of this program was to demonstrate the advantages of using commercial derivative engines and acquisition techniques to satisfy military requirements. The F-117-PW-100 is a derivative of the commercially available Pratt & Whitney PW2037/2040 engines. The military engine performance was established using a commercial specification that was as consistent as possible to the C-17 aircraft performance requirements. Each PW F-117 is capable of producing 41,700 pounds of thrust, although the engine has been qualified to 43,000 pounds of thrust. The F-117 engine is an outgrowth of the successful Pratt & Whitney PW 2000 series engines. The PW 2037 engine received FAA certification in 1983, and entered commercial airline service on the Boeing 757 in 1984. The PW2040 received FAA certification in 1987, and began operations on the Boeing 757PF that year. In 1980, McDonnell Douglas Aircraft (now Boeing) selected the F-117 to power the Globemaster III. The first military version of the PW2040, the F-117 started ground testing in 1988, and after a successful ground testing period, the first flight test engine was delivered to the USAF in 1989. First flight on the C-17 was accomplished in 1991. The first operational engine was delivered for service to the USAF in 1993. Initial operating capability was reached in 1995. Engines for the first three C-17 aircraft production lot's were purchased as Contractor Furnished Equipment. This provided the contractors with the ability to improve engine performance, maintainability, reliability, etc. The engines later reverted to Government Furnished Equipment starting with the fourth aircraft production lot, in November of 1992. The government then took over responsibility for engine performance. The engine also powers versions of the Russian

IL-96M transport. It incorporates a directed flow thrust reverser system, which is deployable in flight as well as on the ground.

Engine Subsystems:

Full Authority Digital Engine Control (FADEC) System: The FADEC System is actually the heart of the engine. This system electronically controls all engine parameters necessary to operate the engine throughout all portions of the flight envelope. The FADEC system acts as what used to be called the main fuel control on older technology jet engines. On the older jet engines the main fuel control was a hydromechanical device, scheduling fuel flow to the engine using mechanical, pneumatic, and hydraulic parameters.

The FADEC system takes this concept further by electronically controlling and scheduling engine operations by interfacing with the flight control system, instrument system, and engine systems to provide for increased engine performance as well as increasing fuel system management, extending aircraft range, and as an added benefit, increasing overall systems reliability. The FADEC is a fully redundant computer, mounted directly on the engine. The FADEC provides virtually a stall free engine operation throughout the aircraft/engine operating envelope.

Electronic Throttle System: The C-17 incorporates an electronic throttle control system, which has taken the place of the old conventional system of mechanical linkages, cables, pulleys, etc. The electronic system has greatly reduced system weight by eliminating all the hardware associated with the mechanical system, and replacing it with an electronic throttle quadrant and associated wiring. An additional advantage over the mechanical system is the increased system reliability and reduction in maintenance manpower required to maintain the system.

The following provides the engine's dimensions and some of its parameters:

Pratt & Whitney F117-PW-100:
  Length   = 146.8 inches
  Diameter   = 84.5 inches
  Weight (Dry)   = 7,100 pounds
  Thrust   = 41,700 pounds
  Specific Fuel Consumption at Maximum Power = 0.34
  Pressure Ratio at Maximum Power = 27.6

The engine is composed of a:
  2 shaft turbofan
  1 single stage 78.5 inch diameter fan with 36
    titanium alloy blades
  4 stage low pressure compressor that rotates with
    the single stage fan
  12 stage high pressure compressor with the
    first 5 stator stages variable
  2 stage high pressure turbine
  5 stage low pressure turbine
  Directed flow thrust reverser system

F-117-PW-100 ENGINE FOLDOUT INTERNAL VIEW
(KEY COMPONENTS)
(Photo credit - Pratt & Whitney)

1. Fan Module Assembly - 78.5 inch diameter

2. Fan - Single stage with 36 solid titanium alloy blades

3. Low Pressure Compressor - 4 stage compressor, rotating
   with fan

4. High Pressure Compressor - 12 stage compressor,
   incorporating vari
   able stator vanes on the first 5 stages, active clearance
   control on the last 8 stages

5. Combustion Chamber - Annular assembly with flame tubes
   manufactured from nickel alloy

6. Single Pipe Fuel Nozzle

7. High Pressure Turbine - 2 stage turbine incorporating
   air cooled
   rotor blades

8. Low Pressure Turbine - 5 stages with active clearance
   control

9. Lubrication Tank

10. Accessory Section

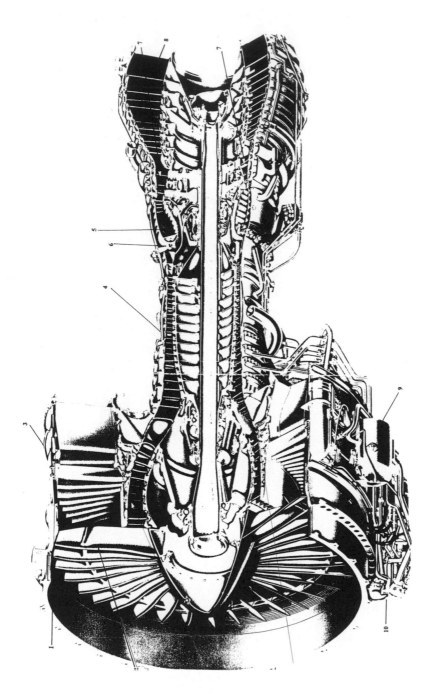

ILLUSTRATION 3. F-117 engine cutaway. (Illustration of Pratt & Whitney). F-117-PO-100 Cutaway View Key Components (Photo credit - Pratt & Whitney)

23. Maintenance on the C-17's four engines is relatively simple, as almost all items are in the open and accessible. (Photo courtesy Pratt & Whitney)

APPENDICIES

APPENDIX I

C-74 Globemaster I Production Contract number AC-27042:

AAF Serial No.	AAF Delivery Date	AAF Retired Date
42-65402	October 1945	October 1954
42-65404	July 1946	May 1954
42-65406	September 1946	September 1954
42-65407	February 1946	July 1954
42-65408	September 1946	October 1954
42-65409	January 1947	October 1954
42-65410	March 1946	March 1954
42-65411	December 1946	September 1953
42-65412	February 1947	October 1954
42-65413	February 1947	February 1954
42-65414	March 1947	February 1954
42-65415	April 1947	January 1954
42-65416 thru 42-65451	Canceled	

C-74 Civilian Conversions:

USAF serial number 42-65408, US civilian registry number N8199. Provided to Panama's Aeronaves de Panama, operated as Panamanian registry number HP-367.

C-74 SPECIFICATIONS

Span:	173 ft. 3 in.
Length:	124 ft. 2 in.
Height:	43 ft. 9 in.
Empty Weight:	86,100 lbs.
Gross Weight:	165,000 lbs.
Alternate Gross Weight:	172,000 lbs.
Engines:	P&W R-4360-49
Fuel Capacity:	11,100 Gal. (Grade 115/145)
Propellers:	Curtis Electric 4 Bladed
Maximum Speed:	325 MPH
Cruise Speed:	296 MPH
Range:	3,400 Miles with 50,000 Pound Payload
Crew:	6 - Pilot, Copilot, Flight Engineer, Navigator, Radio Operator, Loadmaster

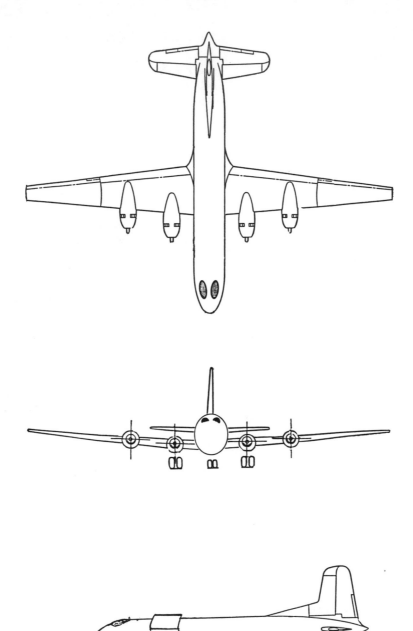

ILLUSTRATION 4. C-74 three view illustration.

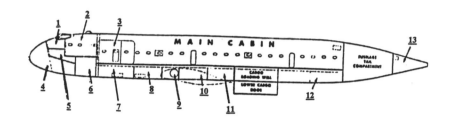

COMPARTMENT LEGEND

1. PILOT & CO-PILOT COMPARTMENTS
2. FLIGHT DECK
3. SIDE LOADING DOOR
4. NOSE WHEEL COMPARTMENT
5. MECHANICAL CONTROLS COMPARTMENT
6. RELIEF CREW COMPARTMENT
7. FORWARD LOWER CARGO COMPARTMENT
8. CENTER LOWER CARGO COMPARTMENT
9. CRAWLWAY COMPARTMENT AND ENTRANCE
10. CENTER WING LOWER CARGO COMPARTMENT
11. AFT LOWER CARGO COMPARTMENT
12. TROOP LADDER STOWAGE COMPARTMENT
13. TAIL CONE COMPARTMENT

ILLUSTRATION 5. C-74 internal compartment illustration.

APPENDIX II

C-124 Globemaster II Production Run Quantities:

YC-124: One produced, rebuilt from C-74 (s/n 42-65406) with redesigned fuselage, clam-shell nose loading doors and four R-4360-49 3,500 horsepower engines

YC-124A: The YC-124's engines were changed to the R-4360-35A, which developed 3,800 horsepower.

C-124A: Douglas model 1129A. Production version with four R-4360-20WA engines developing 3,500 horsepower per engine. 204 were built, which were later retrofitted with the ASP-42 nose radar and wingtip fairing heaters. The following are the contractor and Military serial numbers:

A/F Serial Number	Quantity	Douglas Number
48-795	1	43160
49-232 thru 49-259	28	43161 thru 43188
50-83 thru 50-118	36	43221 thru 43256
50-1255 thru 50-1268	14	43277 thru 43290
51-73 thru 51-182	110	43407 thru 43516
51-5173 thru 51-5187	15	43583 thru 43597

YC-124B: Douglas model 1182E. One prototype built (AF serial number 51-72, contractor number 43406). See variants section for more information on this aircraft.

C-124C: Douglas model 1317. 243 were built, these were re-engined with four 3,800 horsepower R-4360-63A engines, combustion wingtip heaters, AN/APS-42 nose radar, and increased fuel capacity. The following are the contractor and Military serial numbers:

A/F Serial No.	Qty	Douglas Number
51-5188 thru 51-5213	26	43598 thru 43623
51-7272 thru 51-7285	14	43724 thru 43737
52-939 thru 52-1089	151	43848 thru 43998
52-1090	1	43999 (canceled)
53-1 thru 53-52	52	
53-53 thru 53-105	(canceled)	

C-124 Civilian Conversions:

There were no civilian conversions of the Globemaster II.

C-124C SPECIFICATIONS

Span:	174 ft. 2 in.
Length:	130 ft.
Height:	48 ft. 3 in.

Empty Wt: 101,052 lbs.
Gross Wt: 185,000 lbs.
Alternate Gross Wt: 194,500 lbs.
Wing Loading: 74 lbs. per sq. ft
Wing Area: 2506 sq. ft.
Aileron Area: 132.4 sq. ft.
Flap Area: 521.4 sq. ft.
Vertical Tail Area: 280.3 sq. ft.
Rudder Area: 185.1 sq. ft.
Horizontal Stabilizer Area: 394.7 sq. ft.
Elevator Area: 285.8 sq. ft.
Power Loading: 12.2 lbs. per Brake Horsepower
Engines: 4 P&W Ea. R-4360-63A
                                           (P&W Model B-6)
Fuel Capacity:Approx. 11,000 gal. (Grade 115/145)
Propellers: 4 Hamilton Standard, 17 ft. Dia. 3Blade
Crew:5 - Pilot, Copilot, Navigator, Flight Engineer,
                                              Loadmaster
Unit Cost: Flyaway cost was about $1,650,000 each.
                                   (early 1950's dollars)

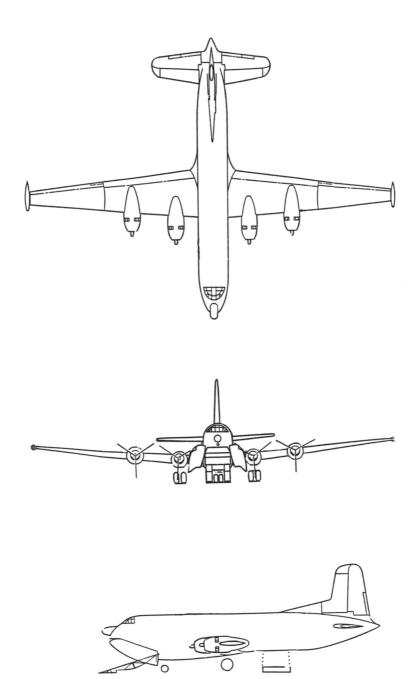

ILLUSTRATION 6. C-124 Three View Illustration.

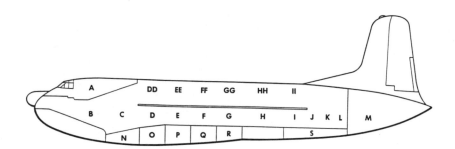

COMPARTMENT LEGEND

A - FLIGHT DECK
B - NOSE LOADING AREA
C THRU L - MAIN CABIN AREA
DD THRU II - UPPER TROOP TRANSPORT SEATING AREA
M - TAIL CONE AREA
N - LOWER DECK AREA
O - LOWER DECK EQUIPMENT AREA, IN LATER C-124C THIS AREA CONTAINED AN APU
P - LOWER DECK EQUIPMENT AREA, CONTAINED HYDRAULIC SYSTEM COMPONENTS, ACCESS TO WING CRAWLWAY
Q THRU S - LOWER DECK STORAGE AREA

COMPARTMENT ALLOWABLE STORAGE WEIGHTS

C - 12,700 POUNDS	G - 10, 000 POUNDS
D - 9,700 POUNDS	H - 9,300 POUNDS
E - 10,000 POUNDS	I - 6,400 POUNDS
F - 10,000 POUNDS	J - 4,800 POUNDS

ILLUSTRATION 7. C-124 Internal Compartments Illustration.

C-124C BASIC AIRCRAFT DIFFERENCES
(AFTER MODIFICATION AND REDESIGNATION 1C-124A-550)

SERIAL NUMBERS AF49-243 THROUGH 50-1268	SERIAL NUMBERS AF51-73 THROUGH 51-132	SERIAL NUMBERS AF51-133 THROUGH 51-182	SERIAL NUMBERS AF51-5173 THROUGH 51-5197	SERIAL NUMBERS AF51-5198 THROUGH 52-1021	SERIAL NUMBERS AF52-1022 AND UP
INDIVIDUAL REFUELING	SINGLE POINT REFUELING	SINGLE POINT REFUELING	SINGLE POINT REFUELING	SINGLE POINT REFUELING	SINGLE POINT REFUELING
HEATERS INTERNAL ONLY	HEATERS INTERNAL & TWO WING TIP PODS	HEATERS INTERNAL & TWO WING TIP PODS	HEATERS INTERNAL & TWO WING TIP PODS	HEATERS INTERNAL & TWO WING TIP PODS	HEATERS INTERNAL & TWO WING TIP PODS
WINDSHIELD DE-ICE (HOT AIR ONLY)	WINDSHIELD DE-ICE (NESA GLASS)	WINDSHIELD DE-ICE (NESA GLASS)	WINDSHIELD DE-ICE (NESA GLASS)	WINDSHIELD DE-ICE (NESA GLASS)	WINDSHIELD DE-ICE (NESA GLASS)
FUEL SYSTEM (6 TANKS)	FUEL SYSTEM (6 TANKS)	FUEL SYSTEM (12 TANKS)	FUEL SYSTEM (12 TANKS)	FUEL SYSTEM (12 TANKS)	FUEL SYSTEM (12 TANKS)
WING FLAPS (FULL SPAN)	WING FLAPS (FULL SPAN)	WING FLAPS (FULL SPAN)	WING FLAPS (PARTIAL SPAN)	WING FLAPS (PARTIAL SPAN)	WING FLAPS (PARTIAL SPAN)
ENGINEERS PANEL FORWARD FACING	ENGINEERS. PANEL FORWARD FACING	ENGINEERS PANEL FORWARD FACING	ENGINEERS. PANEL FORWARD FACING	ENGINEERS. PANEL SIDE FACING	ENGINEERS. PANEL SIDE FACING
AUXILIARY POWER (TWO APP's)	AUXILIARY POWER (TWO APP's)	AUXILIARY POWER (TWO APP's)	AUXILIARY POWER (TWO APP's)	AUXILIARY POWER (TWO APP's)	AUXILIARY POWER (ONE APU)

C-124 CLASS A MISHAP SUMMARY

2 March 1956 - C-124C, serial number 53-021: Enroute from Keflavik, Iceland to Goose Bay Labrador. After 1 hour and 28 minutes of flight, pilot reported returning to Keflavik due to loss of number 2 engine. Seven minutes later pilot declared "MAYDAY" stating engines number 1 and 3 were going out. Thirteen minutes later pilot reported flying at 3,000 feet above water and on only one engine. This was the last report, rescue crews later recovered aircraft debris in water. Seventeen fatalities.

6 April 1956 - C-124A, serial number 51-79: Departed Travis AFB, California for a local maintenance check flight. After climbing to 150 feet, aircraft stalled and fell to the ground. Aircraft destroyed with 3 fatalities, 4 major injuries.

17 April 1956 - C-124A, serial number 50-090: Departed Lockbourne AFB Ohio for Harmon AFB, Newfoundland. After 1 hour and 30 minutes of flight, crew reported fuel fumes in lower equipment compartment. Aircraft diverted to Hamilton, Canada for emergency landing. Concerned over the potential for explosion or fire, the pilot shut down numbers 3 and 4 engines. Once in the pattern to land at Harmon, aircraft main gear did not extend. Pilot raised the nose gear, and performed a gear up landing, which resulted in no injuries, aircraft was destroyed.

16 June 1956 - C-124A, serial number 51-5183: Departed Kwajalein Atoll for Eniwetok Atoll. The aircraft landed 421 feet short of the runway threshold boundary, 8 feet below runway elevation, bounced into the air the contacted the ground just short of the runway and burst into flames, skidding down the runway. No injuries were reported, aircraft was destroyed.

16 August 1956 - C-124A, serial number 51-156: Departed Patrick AFB, Florida for San Salvador. On final to San Salvador, approaching the runway, the right gear struck a 124 foot tall sea wall at the runways end. The aircraft settled on the right wing and slid down the runway until the it came to a stop, turned approximately 145 degrees from the runway heading. The aircraft was destroyed, passengers and crew sustained 1 fatality, 2 major, and 10 minor injuries.

21 August 1956 - C-124C, serial number 52-1005: Departed Palm Beach AFB, Florida for a local transition training flight. Upon executing a training missed approach a loud explosion was heard and the scanner reported the number 2 engine appeared have lost a prop cuff or blade. The engineer reported that number 2 and 3 engine throttles kicked back. The number 2 engine was feathered, the engineer noted that number 3 engine was not producing power. As this unfolded, the instructor pilot took command of the aircraft and placed it in a shallow bank to the right in an attempt to avoid a heavily populated area. The aircraft started a gradual descent which continued until it stalled at approximately 50 feet from the ground. The aircraft was destroyed, there were 3 fatal and 3 major injuries.

3 October 1956 - C-124C, serial number 53-033: Departed Kindley AB, Bermuda bound for Charleston AFB, South Carolina. The weather at Charleston had deteriorated, and as the aircraft passed GCA minimums it clipped the tops of tress that stood about 65 feet above the ground. This caused the loss of power on the number 3 engine, which was feathered by the engineer. The pilot initiated a go around, and due to weather lost sight of the field. GCA reestablished communications with the aircraft 18 miles from the field. In the final last seconds of the flight the co-pilot advised the pilot that the aircraft was lined up for a landing on a highway.

The aircraft crashed on the airfield in an extremely right wing down condition. The aircraft was destroyed, aircrew sustained 1 fatal and 6 major injuries.

27 January 1957 - C-124A, serial number 50-088: Departed Elmendorf AFB, Alaska for McChord AFB, Washington. After takeoff, at 4000 feet, the pilot felt a definite lag in power and then felt and heard violent backfiring on the left side of the aircraft. The engineer reported the number 2 engine backfiring, the scanner reported the engine on fire, which lead to the engineer feathering it. An emergency was declared, and the aircraft started an immediate return to the field. At 2,000 feet the number 3 engine started backfiring, and the engineer reduced power to it. Engines 1 and 4 power were increased to maintain flight. Due to weather, the aircrew could not see the field, and decided to ditch into the sea. It contacted the water a mile and a half off the end of the runway, with a single impact and gradual deceleration. All 13 crew and passengers evacuated the aircraft, no injuries were reported. Only one man fell into the water during evacuation. Aircraft later sank.

22 February 1957 - C-124A, serial number 51-141: Departed Kimpo AB, Korea for Tachikawa AB, Japan. After take-off, and upon reaching climb power, the number 3 engine started backfiring, subsequently explosions were heard, and the engine caught fire. The engineer feathered the engine, and the pilot declared an emergency and started to return to base. Parts of the exploding engine flew into the lower "P" compartment and struck hydraulic system components. The pilot subsequently lost aileron control, and at the same time the engineer reported a loss of power on number 4 engine. Maximum power was applied to number 1 and 2 engines, the pilot and co-pilot maintained wings level with the use of full rudder trim. The aircraft crash landed into a river, with the landing gear in the up position. The aircraft was destroyed. There were 3 fatal, 3 major, and 4 minor injuries.

2 April 1957 - C-124A, serial number 51-5176: Aircraft departed Churchill Canadian Base for Cambridge Bay Canadian Base. On final approach to Cambridge Bay, the aircraft touched down in a normal landing attitude short of the runway on a gravel strip, and struck a gravel embankment. The impact separated both wings with the left wing exploding on impact and the fuselage skidded approximately 650 feet down the runway. It came to rest balanced on its nose landing gear. The aircraft was destroyed, there were no serious injuries.

31 August 1957 - C-124C, serial number 52-1021: Departed Hunter AFB, Georgia for Biggs AFB, Texas. Weather at Biggs was the controlling factor in this mishap. Visibility was 3 miles with thunderstorms and rainshowers. The last transmission reported by the pilot was that he was over the outer marker.
A large ball of fire was observed approximately 2 miles from the airport. The aircraft struck the ground and was destroyed. Of the 15 aboard, 5 received fatal injuries, 9 major injuries, and 1 minor injuries.

4 September 1957 - C-124A, serial number 51-5173: Departed Larson AFB, Minnesota for Broome County Airport, New York. During flare out at Broome airport, the pilot and co-pilot reportedly felt the aircraft sinking into a downdraft. The aircraft struck an embankment at the end of the runway, breaking in half and skidding down the runway. The right wing exploded, and the aircraft came to rest in flames. Of the 9 on board, 7 received major injuries, 2 minor injuries. The aircraft was destroyed.

28 November 1957 - C-124C, serial number 52-995: Departed Wheelus AB, Algeria for Esenboga Airport, Turkey.

Weather at Esenboga deteriorated, after passing the outer marker the co-pilot reported visual contact with the runway. Due to a ragged ceiling the crew lost visual with the runway upon entering clouds. The pilot call a missed approach, maximum power was applied to the engines. However, the aircraft struck rolling terrain approximately 6 miles from the airport. The aircraft disintegrated during contact with the ground, ending up with the flight deck compartment inverted. There were 3 fatalities, 3 major injuries, and 1 survived without injuries.

7 January 1958 - C-124C, serial number 53-0036: Departed Brookley AFB, Alabama for a local transition training flight. During a maximum power go-around the number 2 propeller ran away. The engineer attempted unsuccessfully to reduce engine rpm, he was also unsuccessful at feathering the propeller. The run away propeller created a significant yaw to the aircraft's flight path. An emergency landing was accomplished. After touchdown the aircraft slid 760 feet. The crew evacuated successfully, however the number 3 engine continued to run for approximately 2 hours, with all the switches turned off. It was eventually shut down by the use of a fire truck spraying foam into the carburetor intake. Although there were no injuries the aircraft was destroyed.

27 March 1958 - C-124C, serial number 52-981: Aircraft sustained a mid-air collision near Fort Worth Texas with a C-119 aircraft. Both aircraft crashed to the ground killing 10 crew members and 5 passengers on the C-124 and 3 crew members on the C-119.

3 June 1958, C-124A, serial number 51-114: Departed Tachikawa AB, Japan for a flight to Honolulu International Airport, Hawaii. On the take-off roll, one or more engines started backfiring, the aircraft became airborne 3,000 feet after computations indicated it should have. At lift-off the number 1 engine carburetor air intake components started to disintegrate, the aircraft started a shallow left turn in an attempt to return to base. The number 1 engine failed and the number 3 engine lost power. Aircraft was unable to sustain flight and crashed, breaking up and was engulfed in flames. The aircraft was destroyed, and 6 crewmembers lost their lives, two additional crewmembers sustained major injuries.

4 July 1958, C-124A, serial number 50-107: Departed Hickam AFB, Hawaii for Wake Island. After 1 hour and 30 minutes of flight the engineer noted number 3 engine cylinder D-6 spark plugs fouling. Defouling procedures were initiated which cleared the plugs. After another hour and a half the number 3 engine started backfiring violently. The pilot ordered the engine feathered and the aircraft started to return to Hickam. The number 3 engine generator light illuminated, the second engineer entered the wing crawlway, climbed out to the number 3 engine and lowered the firewall door to inspect the generator which he found to be cool to the touch. Upon climbing back into the aircraft he noted that the number 3 engine propeller was still turning and that the engine was leaking oil, he reported this to the engineer. The propeller continued to turn, creating drag on the aircraft. With the inability to feather the number 3 engine the pilot decided to divert to Johnston Island, the nearest airfield. Eighteen minutes later the number 3 propeller separated from the engine and struck the fuselage, opening a large hole in the side of the main cabin. It also severed aileron control as well as number 4 engine controls, and all electrical power. The aircraft could not sustain flight and crash landed in the water where it broke apart upon contact. Four crewmembers were listed as missing, three crewmembers were recovered and sustained major injuries.

2 September 1958, C-124C, serial number 52-1081: Departed Agana NAS, Guam for Clark AB, Philippines. Contact with the aircraft was lost shortly after take-off. Two hours later search and rescue vessels reported an oil slick on the oceans surface. None of the 7 crewmembers were recovered. Aircraft was presumed lost at sea.

17 September 1958, C-124A, serial number 51-0165: Departed Donaldson AFB, South Carolina for Travis AFB, California. Near Tulsa, Oklahoma the number 4 engine was noted to have high fuel flow. The engine was feathered, and the second engineer entered the crawlway to inspect for a possible fuel leak. None was noted and the engine was restarted. The flight plan was changed to have the aircraft land at Tinker AFB, Oklahoma for inspection. Upon final approach to Tinker, pilot reported aircraft yawed to the right, it subsequently veered to the right, away from the runway. He raised the gear and started a go-around, however before gaining altitude the right wing struck the ground. The aircraft broke up and was engulfed in flames. The aircraft was destroyed, one crewmember died, 7 crewmembers sustained major injuries.

16 October 1958, C-124C, serial number 52-1017: Departed Christchurch, New Zealand for an airdrop mission to McMurdo Sound, Antarctica. Navigational error near Cape Hellett Bay cause the aircraft to fly into a 3200 foot mountain. The aircraft was destroyed, all 7 crewmembers lost their lives.

11 January 1959, C-124A, serial number 50-111: Departed McChord AFB, Washington for Kodiak NAS, Alaska. Approximately 2 hours and 30 minutes into the flight the number 1 engine was feathered due to a "dead cylinder". Approximately 1 hour and 30 minutes later the number 3 engine was feathered for a generator overheat condition. The destination was then changed to Homer, Alaska, the nearest airfield. Nearing Homer the pilot reported his position and altitude, the altitude reported to be 5,200 feet. Homer immediately informed the crew of a 5,224 foot mountain within the immediate area. Contact was lost with the aircraft when it flew into the mountain. Eight crewmembers lost their lives.

31 March 1959, C-124C, serial number 51-5201: Departed Incirlik AB, Turkey for Esenboga AB, Turkey. Aircraft attempted take-off at high gross weight without ADI injection and with engine blowers set at high output. This combination resulted in low engine power output. Shortly after lift-off the landing gear was raised, and the pilot noted the aircraft had insufficient airspeed to maintain flight. The aircraft's right wing struck the ground first, and upon fuselage contact the aircraft was engulfed in flames, and disintegrated. There were 2 fatalities, 6 with major injuries, and one with minor injuries.

6 July 1959, C-124A, serial number 49-0254: Departed Barksdale AFB, Louisiana for Little Rock AFB, Arkansas. During take-off run engines 1 and 4 were reported to be backfiring. The engines continued to backfire throughout remainder of flight. At 50 to 100 feet above ground the aircraft was observed to level off, then the aircraft settled back into the ground. Aircraft was destroyed, no injuries were sustained to the crew.

18 April 1960, C-124C, serial number 52-1062: Departed Ernest Harmon AFB, Newfoundland for Lajes Air Station, Azores. Approximately 2 minutes after take-off the aircraft struck the top of a 450 foot hill 2 miles from the runway. It then made contact with a second hill, flew between 2 more hills, and crashed at the edge of a nearby lake approximately 3 miles from the base. Communications was lost with the aircraft shortly after take-off. The aircraft exploded and burned upon final contact with the ground. All 9 aboard died.

19 June 1960, C-124C, serial number 52-993: Departed Patrick AFB, Florida for Recife, Brazil. Upon let down at final destination weather deteriorated, the aircraft flew into several large trees and disintegrated, fire subsequently consumed the aircraft. The aircraft was completely destroyed. There were 3 fatalities, 3 sustained major injuries, and one walked away without any injuries.

9 January 1961, C-124C, serial number 52-969: Departed Lajes AB, Azores for Spangdahlem AB, Germany. On final into Spangdahlem aircraft contacted trees near the end of the runway, subsequently the right wing contacted the ground and separated from the aircraft. The aircraft, then on the ground, turned 180 degrees, the tail section separated from the fuselage and the aircraft was subsequently consumed by fire. Of the 15 aboard, 3 received major injuries with the remaining receiving minor injuries.

24 May 1961, C-124A, serial number 51-0174: Departed McChord AFB, Washington for Fort Sill, Oklahoma. Approximately 1 minute and 14 seconds after take-off the aircraft crashed 2 miles south of the runway, cause unknown. All 22 aboard perished.

24 May 1962, C-124A, serial number 51-147: Departed Tachikawa AB, Japan for local night transition flight. Aircraft performed several touch and go landings at Yokota AB, Japan. Approximately 5 minutes after the last touch and go at Yokota the aircraft crashed, cause unknown. All 7 crewmembers aboard perished.

2 January 1964, C-124C, serial number 52-968: Departed Wake Island for Honolulu Airport. Aircraft disappeared after approximately 7 hours of flight, cause of disappearance unknown, all 9 crewmembers aboard lost at sea.

22 January 1965, C-124C, serial number 52-1058: Departed Aviano, Italy for Athens, Greece. Aircraft crashed into the side of Mt. Helmos, Turkey at an elevation of 6850 feet, Mt. Helmos elevation is 7402 feet. Cause appeared to be navigational aid problems. All 10 crewmembers aboard perished.

24 March 1965, C-124C, serial number 52-1075: Departed Dover, Delaware for a routine local VFR/IFR proficiency flight. After several hours of training flights the right wing of the aircraft separated outboard of the number 4 engine. The aircraft crashed near Cordova, Maryland. All 6 crewmembers perished.

12 February 1966, C-124C, serial number 52-980: Departed San Javier Airport, Spain for Moron AB, Spain. Nine minutes after take-off the last transmission was heard from the aircraft, with the pilot reporting the aircraft's position. Aircraft crashed and was completely destroyed, cause unknown. All 8 crewmembers perished.

24 June 1967, C-124C, serial number 50-86: Departed Richards-Gebaur AFB, Missouri for Whiteman AFB, Missouri on a routine training flight. Upon landing at Whiteman the pilot placed the propellers in reverse pitch, looked down at the instrument panel, and the aircraft veered left. The instructor pilot aboard advanced the number 1 throttle in an attempt to realign the aircraft on the runway. The aircraft did not response so a Max-power go-around was commanded. The number 1 and 4 propellers overspead. Aircraft drifted left and became airborne. The Instructor Pilot ordered engines 1 and 4 feathered. Immediately after the number 4 propeller stopped rotating the Instructor Pilot ordered the number 4 engine restarted. The engine rpm would not increase above 1,000 rpm. The airspeed bled off to 80 knots, the aircraft stalled and contacted the ground wings level, tail low. After sliding approximately 400 feet, the number 3 propeller and gearing broke off the engine.

The fuselage broke apart and a fire started at the number 3 engine. The aircraft was destroyed by the subsequent fire. The 6 crewmembers escaped without injuries.

28 July 1968, C-124C, serial number 51-5178: Departed Zanderrij, Surinam for Guarapapes, Brazil. Upon letdown nearing Guarapapes, the aircraft impacted the top of an 1890 foot hill 51 miles from its final destination. The aircraft was destroyed, all 10 crewmembers aboard perished.

26 August 1970, C-124C, serial number 52-1049: Departed McChord AFB, Washington for Cold Bay, Alaska. Aircraft impacted the 8,215 foot tall Pavolf Volcano in Alaska. Weather appeared to be a factor. The aircraft was completely destroyed, and all 7 crewmembers aboard perished.

3 May 1972, C-124C, serial number 52-1055: Departed Galeao International Airport for Zanderij Airport, Surinam. During the last 5 minutes of flight the pilot reported he was not receiving normal indications from the Zanderij navigational site. The airport control tower lost contact with the aircraft. The wreckage was discovered later in the day. The aircraft had impacted at the 1650 foot level of a 1716 foot hill, 42.5 miles from its destination. The aircraft was completely destroyed, all 8 crewmembers perished.

APPENDIX III

C-17A Specifications

Crew:
Three - Pilot, Co-Pilot, and Loadmaster. Provisions on flight deck for seating two observers.

Flight Controls:
Digital Fly By Wire, incorporating quad redundant flight control computers with mechanical back-up.

External Dimensions:
Wing Span (total including winglets) = 169.8ft.Wing Area = 3,800 sq. ft.
Wing Type = Supercritical airfoil, 25 degree sweep.
Length = 174 ft.
Height = 55.1 ft.
Fuselage Diameter 22.5ft.

Internal Dimensions:
Cargo Compartment Loadable Width = 13.5 ft.
Cargo Compartment Height = 13.5 ft. (11.8ft under wing crossover)
Rear Cargo Ramp Loading Width = 18 ft.
Rear Cargo Ramp Loading Length = 19.8 ft.

Weights:
Empty Operating Weight = 277,000 lbs.
Typical Payload Weight = 120,000 lbs.
Heavy Payload Weight = 150,000 lbs.
Maximum Payload Weight = 169,000 lbs.
Maximum Take-Off Weight = 580,000 lbs.
Rear Cargo Ramp Weight = 8,000 lbs.

Powerplant:
   4 P&W F117-PW-100 turbofans (P&W Model 2040)

Unit Cost:
   Flyaway cost is approximately $175,000,000 each.
   (early 1990's dollars).

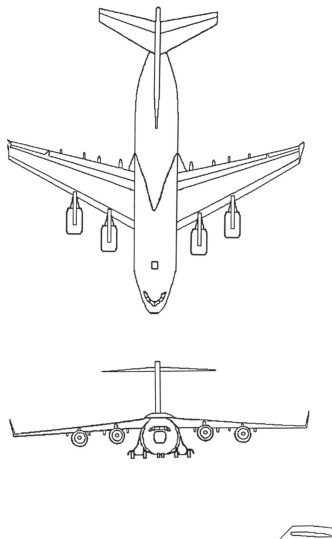
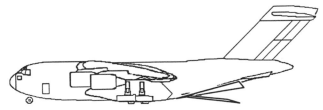

ILLUSTRATION 9. C-17 Three View Illustration

Production Run Quantities:

F\Year	Purchase	Lot #	Quantity	Production #	USAF Serial #
	Prototype	1	1	T-1	87-0025
1988	1	2	2	P-1 thru P-2	88-0265 thru 88-0266
1989	2	4	4	P-3 thru P-6	89-1189 thru 89-1192
1990	3	4	4	P-7 thru P-10	90-0532 thru 90-0535
1991	None	None	None		
1992	4	4	4	P-11 thru P-14	92-3291 thru 92-3294
1993	5	6	6	P-15 thru P-20	93-0599 thru 93-0604
1994	6	6	6	P-21 thru P-26	94-0065 thru 94-0070
1995	7	6	6	P-27 thru P-32	95-0102 thru 95-0107
1996	8	8	8	P-33 thru P-39	96-0001 thru 96-0007
1997	9	8	8	P-40 thru P-49	
1998	10	9	9	P-50 thru P-51	
1999	11	13	13	P-52 thru P-64	
2000	12	15	15	P-65 thru P-79	
2001	13	15	15	P-80 thru P-94	
2002	14	15	15	P-95 thru P-109	
2003	15	5	5	P-110 thru P-114	

Assignments:

97th Air Mobility Wing, Altus AFB, Oklahoma - Eight C-17A aircraft. Replacing the nine Lockheed C-141 Starlifter's that were retired from service.

The 67th Air Mobility Wing, McChord AFB, Washington - Forty Eight C-17A's. Replacing the C-141 retired from service.

The 437th Air Mobility Wing, Charleston AFB, SC - Forty Eight C-17A's. Replacing retiring C-141 aircraft.

Remaining procurement of aircraft proposed assigned to special operations missions.

C-17 Dedication Names:

Aircraft	Name
P-1 / 88-0265	The City of Altus
P-6 / 89-1192	The Spirit of Charleston
P-27 / 95-0102	The Spirit of Long Beach
P-31 / 95-0106	The Spirit of Bob Hope
P-32 / 95-0107	The Spirit of North Charleston
P-34 / 96-0002	The Spirit of the Air Force
P-37 / 96-0005	The Spirit of Sgt. John L. Levitow
P-38 / 96-0006	The Spirit of Berlin
P-39 / 96-0007	The Spirit of America's Veteran's
P-40 / 96-0008	The Spirit of the Total Force

Future Dedications:

The Spirit of Tuskegee (Tuskegee Airmen)
The Spirit of Maryland (Andrews AFB, MD)
The Spirit of the Northwest (Seattle/Tacoma McChord AFB)
The Spirit of Mississippi (172 Airlift Wing, Jackson MS)
The Spirit of Fayetteville (Ft. Bragg/Pope AFB, NC)
The Spirit of Jimmy Stewart

Acknowledgments

The author recognizes that some words, model names and designations mentioned in this book are the property of the trademark holder, and are used as identification only. This is not an official publication. The author wishes to thank each of the following individuals and organizations for the contribution of time, information, and vast amounts of patients which has made this book possible.

United Technologies Corporation
Pratt & Whitney Division
Hamilton Standard Division

The Smithsonian Institution

Department of the Air Force
Air Force Historical Research Agency
Maxwell Air Force Base, Alabama
Especially Archives Branch Department

Director De Aeronautica Civil
Director De Seguridad Aerea, Panama

The Boeing Company
Douglas Products Division
Historical Archives

USAF Safety Center
Kirtland Air Force Base, New Mexico

And Especially the Travis Air Base Museum, for their assistance in providing access to an exceptionally well restored C-124C. Thanks for all the time spent with me, and for bringing back precious memories.

Index

The history of military air transport to date has been incomplete. Lacking is the document legacy of two relatively unknown Douglas transports, the reciprocating engined Globemaster I and II. These propeller driven aircraft set the benchmark for the heavy lift transport's that are currently in operation in both civilian and military service.

Lost in history is the fact that Globemaster I was the first truly heavy lift transport to enter military service. Its offspring, the Globemaster II, for over twenty years performed yeoman's work in supporting not only the US and its allies, but also provided humanitarian relief to the world at large.